Wake Tech． T4-ADN-600
9101 Fayetteville Road
Raleigh, North Carolina 27603-5696

WITHDRAWN

Music Library Association
Index and Bibliography Series
Mark Palkovic, Series Editor

1. *An Alphabetical Index to Claudio Monteverdi Tutte Le Opere,* edited by the Bibliography Committee of the New York Chapter, MLA, 1964.
2. *An Alphabetical Index to Hector Berlioz Werke,* edited by the Bibliography Committee of the New York Chapter, MLA, 1964.
3. *A Checklist of Music Bibliographies and Indexes in Progress and Unpublished,* compiled by the MLA Publications Committee Walter Gerboth, chair; Shirley Branner; and James B. Coover; 1965; 2nd ed. by James Pruett, 1969; 3rd ed. by Linda Solow, 1974; 4th ed. by Dee Baily, 1982.
4. *A Concordance of the Thematic Indexes to the Instrumental Works of Antonio Vivaldi,* by Lenore Coral, 1965; 2nd ed., 1972.
5. *An Alphabetical Index to Tomás Luis de Victoria Opera Omnia,* edited by the Bibliography Committee of the New York Chapter, MLA, 1966.
6. *An Alphabetical Index to Robert Schumann Werke: Schumann Index, Part 1,* compiled by Michael Ochs, 1967.
7. *An Alphabetical Index to the Solo Songs of Robert Schumann: Schumann Index, Part 2,* compiled by William J. Weichlein, 1967.
8. *An Index to Maurice Frost's "English & Scottish Psalm & Hymn Tunes,"* by Kirby Rogers, 1967.
9. *Speculum: An Index of Musically Related Articles and Book Reviews,* compiled by Arthur S. Wolff, 1970; 2nd ed., 1981.
10. *An Index to "Das Chorwerk," Vols. 1–110,* compiled by Michael Ochs, 1970.
11. *Bach Aria Index,* compiled by Miriam Whaples, 1971.
12. *Annotated Bibliography of Writing about Music in Puerto Rico,* compiled by Annie Figueroa Thompson, 1975.
13. *Analyses of Twentieth-Century Music, 1940–1970,* compiled by Arthur Wenk, 1975.
14. *Analyses of Twentieth-Century Music, 1970–1975,* compiled by Arthur Wenk, 1976; 2nd ed., 1984.
15. *Analyses of Nineteenth-Century Music: 1940–1975,* compiled by Arthur Wenk, 1976; 2nd ed., *1940–1980,* 1984.
16. *Writings on Contemporary Music Notation,* compiled by Gerald Warfield, 1976.
17. *Literature for Voices in Combination with Electronic and Tape Music: An Annotated Bibliography,* compiled by J. Michele Edwards, 1977.

18. *Johannes Brahms: A Guide to His Autographs in Facsimile,* by Peter Dedel, 1978.
19. *Source: Music of the Avant Garde; Annotated List of Contents and Cumulative Indices,* by Michael D. Williams, 1978.
20. *Eighteenth-Century American Secular Music Manuscripts: An Inventory,* compiled by James J. Fuld and Mary Wallace Davidson, 1980.
21. *Popular Secular Music in America through 1800: A Checklist of Manuscripts in North American Collections,* compiled by Kate Van Winkle Keller, 1980.
22. *Palestrina: An Index to the Casimiri, Kalmus, and Haberl Editions,* by Allison Hall, 1980.
23. *E. H. Fellowes: An Index to The English Madrigalists and The English School of Lutenist Song Writers,* by Allison Hall, 1984.
24. *Music in New York during the American Revolution: An Inventory of Musical References in "Rivington's New York Gazette,"* by Gillian B. Anderson with editorial assistance by Neil Ratliff, 1987.
25. *Analyses of Nineteenth- and Twentieth-Century Music, 1940–1985,* by Arthur B. Wenk, 1987.
26. *Opera Performances in Video Format: A Checklist of Commercially Released Performances,* by Charles Croissant, 1991.
27. *A Thematic Catalog of the Works of Robert Valentine,* by J. Bradford Young, 1994.
28. *Pro-Musica: Patronage, Performance, and a Periodical—An Index to the Quarterlies,* by Paula Elliot, 1997.
29. *Musical Memorials for Musicians: A Guide to Selected Compositions,* by R. Michael Fling, 2001.
30. *Music Inspired by Art: A Guide to Recordings,* by Gary Evans, 2002.
31. *An Index to Music Published in* The Etude *Magazine, 1883-1957,* by E. Douglas Bomberger, 2004.
32. *Bibliographic Control of Music, 1897–2000,* by Richard P. Smiraglia, compiled and edited with J. Bradford Young, 2006.

Bibliographic Control of Music, 1897–2000

Richard P. Smiraglia

compiled and edited with
J. Bradford Young

*Music Library Association
Index and Bibliography Series, No. 32*

The Scarecrow Press, Inc.
Lanham, Maryland • Toronto • Oxford
and
Music Library Association, Inc.
2006

SCARECROW PRESS, INC.

Published in the United States of America
by Scarecrow Press, Inc.
A wholly owned subsidiary of
The Rowman & Littlefield Publishing Group, Inc.
4501 Forbes Boulevard, Suite 200, Lanham, Maryland 20706
www.scarecrowpress.com

PO Box 317
Oxford
OX2 9RU, UK

Copyright © 2006 by Richard P. Smiraglia

All rights reserved. No part of this publication may be reproduced, stored in a retrieval system, or transmitted in any form or by any means, electronic, mechanical, photocopying, recording, or otherwise, without the prior permission of the publisher.

British Library Cataloguing in Publication Information Available

Library of Congress Cataloging-in-Publication Data
Smiraglia, Richard P., 1952–
 Bibliographic control of music, 1897–2000 / Richard P. Smiraglia ; compiled and edited with J. Bradford Young.
  p. cm. — (Music Library Association index and bibliography series ; no. 32)
 Includes indexes.
 ISBN-13: 978-0-8108-5133-7 (alk. paper)
 ISBN-10: 0-8108-5133-4 (alk. paper)
  1. Cataloging of music–Bibliography. 2. Cataloging of sound recordings–Bibliography. 3. Classification–Music–Bibliography. 4. Classification–Sound recordings–Bibliography. I. Young, J. Bradford. II. Title. III. MLA index and bibliography series ; 32.
ML111.S596 2006
016.0253'48–dc22   2005056357

♾ The paper used in this publication meets the minimum requirements of American National Standard for Information Sciences—Permanence of Paper for Printed Library Materials, ANSI/NISO Z39.48-1992.
Manufactured in the United States of America.

Contents

List of Tables	vii
Preface	ix
Acknowledgments	xi
Introduction	1
From James Duff Brown (1897) to Arsen Ralph Papakhian (2000): An Essay on the Literature of the Bibliographic Control of Music	5
Bibliographic Control of Music, 1897-2000: Chronological Listing	31
Title Index	89
Author Index	115
Keyword Index	133
Journal Index	137
About the Authors	145

Tables

1.	Undated Local Classifications	9
2.	Frequency of Keywords	14
3.	Year of First Occurence of Keyword	15
4.	Author Productivity	17
5.	Author Productivity by Keyword	20
6.	Authors in Academic, Public and Discography Groups	21
7.	Journal Productivity	23

Preface

This project has a long and colorful history, at least for a bibliography. In 1983 after publishing the first edition of my manual *Cataloging Music: A Manual for Use with AACR2* (Soldier Creek Press) I had the good fortune to meet a representative of the publishing house that was known as Libraries Unlimited. As we spoke about the possibilities for a book on music cataloging, I had the sense that there was really quite a lot more that could be said about the subject than I had been able to cover in the Soldier Creek manual or in the *Shelflisting Music* manual that I had published with the Music Library Association (1981). In fact, it was clear to me at the time that there was extensive if somewhat scattered literature about music cataloging. In particular, I was aware that many early music librarians had documented their work as they participated in the development of cataloging codes, subject heading lists, and so forth. So I set out to produce the book that became *Music Cataloging: The Bibliographic Control of Printed and Recorded Music in Libraries* (Libraries Unlimited, 1989).

Notwithstanding my excitement at having landed an honest-to-goodness book contract, I was somewhat frightened of the prospect that I might miss something along the way. I had not yet begun studying for my Ph.D., itself a terrifying process, during which I would be taught how to cover a subject exhaustively and exhaustingly. I was fortunate to obtain grant funds from the Research Board of the University of Illinois at Urbana–Champaign, with which I was able to hire a series of graduate assistants to compile the bibliography from which I hoped to write my book.

Beginning in 1983 and proceeding over the next four years or so, graduate assistants from various sources worked to compile an exhaustive bibliography on music cataloging. Quite a lot of the work was done

x   Preface

from manual indexes, of course, including an excellent bibliography of early literature compiled by David Hunter from Cannons's *Bibliography of Library Economy* 1876-1920, *Library Literature* 1921-1982, *Music Index* 1949-1976, and *Library and Information Science Abstracts* 1969-1981. This was supplemented eventually with online searches, which in those days had to be mediated, and the whole thing was entered laboriously into an early word processor and printed out by an under-inked dot-matrix printer on that wonderful striped green-and-white computer paper with perforated pages. Later, as I actually prepared the book, I would send graduate assistants in search of copies of specific articles that would figure in the text. And like most scholars I would chase down references from the reference lists of the documents I was reading until the bibliography grew like Topsy.

And then it sat in my office for a very long time. At various intervals I would shake my head and say what a shame nothing had come of all this work, and yet other priorities always seemed to outweigh any effort I might undertake to complete this bibliography. In the introduction to *Music Cataloging* I had commented on my observation that the literature betrayed a surprising tendency for succeeding generations to reinvent various wheels, mostly having to do with cataloging sound recordings, apparently completely unaware of the literature and standards that had been produced by their predecessors. This comment caught the attention of Brad Young, who, along with other professional acquaintances, suggested that this bibliography ought to be resurrected, completed, and published for the use of students of music librarianship. And so the current project was born.

Which led, of course, to the employ of a new generation of graduate assistants, this time from the Palmer School of Library and Information Science at Long Island University. Oddly, none of my assistants at The School of Library Service at Columbia University, where I actually wrote *Music Cataloging*, worked on this project. This new cadre was employed to scan the original bibliography to produce a Microsoft Word copy of the original bibliography, to search online indexes to update it, and then to enter the copy into ProCite so it could be edited and analyzed for this publication. Finally, Brad Young contributed the time of his assistant at the University of Pennsylvania to complete fact-checking of the manuscript.

Richard P. Smiraglia

Acknowledgments

The present document is the product of the labors of the following students over a period of nearly twenty years, without whom this publication would not have been possible:

Douglas Salokar, Karen Lanz, David Hunter, Alan Hoffman, Constance Wernersbach, Dean Jensen—from the University of Illinois; and,

Kenichi Tsuda, Ed Scarcelle, Matthew F. Ainsworth, Alon Friedman—from Long Island University; and,

Michael F. Berry—from the University of Pennsylvania.

Our thanks, in most cases much belated to all of these folks. In gratitude for their work, and in the hopes that this publication will be used by future students of music librarianship, we have asked the proceeds from this publication be directed to the Music Library Association's Kevin Freeman Fund to be used as scholarship opportunities for students to attend and participate in meetings of the Music Library Association.

Introduction

This volume contains a retrospective bibliography of the literature of the bibliographic control of music. Although systematic efforts to develop and organize music collections in libraries are known to have been made for nearly 600 years, their documentation is scant and scattered. The purpose of this project is to support historical and theoretical research into the organization of music in libraries. Many current standards have evolved from earlier practices with little understanding of the context in which they arose. The consequence, apparent in the findings of this project (Smiraglia 1989, p. xii), is that each generation has endeavored to reinvent the work of the preceding within an unnecessary philosophical vacuum. Beyond understanding the origins of current practice, earlier literature provides a basis on which to formulate theoretical paradigms that can be tested and used to articulate principles. Furthermore, bibliometric measures based on the subject bibliography of specific communities can be used to describe evolutionary patterns, which in turn point to the development of theoretical paradigms. This bibliography should serve to illuminate the music information profession, both its history and future.

The text comprises a select bibliography of 880 periodical and monographic citations for professional and scholarly literature relevant to the organization of music in libraries. General library administration is excluded. Any language, place, date or format of publication has been included. Relevant items were identified in standard bibliographies and indices such as *Library Literature*, *Music Index*, and so forth. Therefore the coverage, although comprehensive, is not exhaustive, particularly of foreign publications, as fugitive literature not reported in standard bibliographic tools will not have been identified. In addition, unpublished research papers directly relevant to the bibliographic control of music were added as they became known. The following bibliographies and indexes were searched to produce this bibliography:

Print Sources

Cannons' *Bibliography of Library Economy* 1876-1920
   Classification—Music
   Cataloguing and Indexing—Music
Library Literature 1921-1982
   Classification—special subject—music
   Music collections
      Cataloging
      Classification
   Music libraries and collections
      Cataloging
      Classification
   Music literature and scores
      Cataloging
      Classification
   Phonograph records
   Subject headings—special subjects—music
Music Index 1949-1976
   Classification
Library and Information Science Abstracts 1969-1981

Online Sources

Library Literature 1982-2001
   Music Cataloging and Classification (162 hits)
   Sound Recordings Cataloging and Classification (31 hits)
   Music-subject
   Collection development
Music Index 1982-2001
RILM Abstracts
   Music cataloging

Collection Development
Subjects
IIMP
Classification and Cataloging
Collection Development
Subjects
Library and Information Science Abstracts 1969-2001
* #1 music and (Classification or Cataloging) and (PY = 1984-2001) (87 records)
* #2 music and (Subject) and (PY = 1984-2001) (184 records)
* #3 music and collection development and (PY = 1984-2001) (38 records)

Editorial Practices

Data are preserved as found in the source of the citations described above with some exceptions. Duplicate citations for the same publication from various sources have been omitted. Punctuation, capitalization and italicization have been edited to conform to the *Chicago Manual of Style*. Personal and corporate names and journal titles have been regularized to facilitate indexing. Initial articles have been omitted from foreign titles. Book reviews have been uniformly cited with a title in the style "Review. etc." Topical keywords have been selectively added for indexing. Edition, series, and thesis statements have been recorded as notes. Translations of foreign-language titles found in the source of the citations have been recorded as notes; for others, a translation has been provided by the editor. For convenience, the various volumes of the *Code international de catalogage de la musique* have been cited individually and as a set.

The main body of the bibliography contains full bibliographic citations in a chronological list. Citations in the main list are numbered sequentially. Indexes are provided, using the citation numbers as pointers, for author's names (based on the first author listed in joint-authorship works), titles, keywords and journal titles. The keyword index uses the following taxonomy, derived from the titles of the individual citations:

Academic libraries
Automation
Book reviews
Cataloging rules
Classification
Descriptive cataloging
Descriptive cataloging rules
Discography
Librettos
MARC
Music librarianship
Musicology
National libraries
Nonbook materials
Public libraries
Retrospective conversion
School libraries
Scores
Sound recordings
Special libraries
Subject headings

Work Cited

Smiraglia, Richard P. 1989. *Music Cataloging: The Bibliographic Control of Printed and Recorded Music in Libraries*. Littleton, Colo.: Libraries Unlimited.

From James Duff Brown (1897) to Arsen Ralph Papakhian (2000): An Essay on the Literature of the Bibliographic Control of Music

In *Bibliographies: Their Aims and Methods* (1984), Donald Krummel suggests that the prime purpose for enumerative bibliography is to provide order over a select segment of an ever expanding world of recorded knowledge. The present bibliography began as background research for a text on music cataloging. But here in its expanded and edited form, this list has become a lively illustration of the story of the development of music librarianship as seen through the lens of bibliographic control. Here this story will be narrated in several different ways. We will look at the chronology of events, at the development of what might be discourse communities contributing variously to the bibliographic control of music, and at the curious scatter of this literature across very broad bibliographical horizons, as demonstrated by analysis of the forms of publication represented here.

The Big Story: Three Issues

The 880 works cited in this bibliography tell the story of music cataloging from the late 19th century until the turn of the present century. The list is arrayed chronologically because it allows the browser to observe the progress of events over that period of time. In general, the sequence moves from concern over the descriptive cataloging of scores, through the rapid development of new musical media, into the age of automated librarianship; our story ends in 2000, roughly at the opening of the current era of the ubiquity of the Internet. Readers will want to bear in mind that our task in this essay is to narrate this bibliography, rather than to tell the complete history of music cataloging (Bradley 2003).

In 1897 James Duff Brown's brief article on the "Cataloguing of Music" illustrated the beginning of the professionalization of the bibliographic control of music materials in libraries. Brown presents a set of issues that will predominate for decades: how to incorporate music into a catalog of books and how to group musical works for retrieval. Three problems predominate in this early period, but these problems—access to works, proper ontology and physical arrangement—will persist even into our own day at the outset of the 21st century.

First, librarians were concerned with how to transcribe the titles of musical works so as to make an effective entry in an author–title catalog. It would be nearly a century later before the complex practice of constructing uniform titles would get codified, to provide a partial resolution to this issue. But the issue would become more complex with the introduction of sound recordings, which were nearly always anthologies. Sound recording catalogers would argue endlessly about whether the whole item should be cataloged or whether it should be each work separately entered into the catalog. Given the structure of catalogs based on Cutter's objectives (1876), this is not a surprise. The famous *Rules for a Dictionary Catalog* assumed a one-to-one correspondence between "work" and "document." This, of course, has never been the case in music collections, where many copies and parts and varying scores of works were held; the problem was even more exaggerated in collections of sound recordings, where each work and every part of each work was held in multiple recordings of multiple performances. It makes the head swim to ponder the chaos. Music librarians were nothing if not pragmatists in these early days, and they did what they needed to do to provide the best access to their collections. Only in the last decade or so have we seen other epistemological approaches applied (Hjørland 1998; Smiraglia 2003; and Vellucci 1997). By the end of the 20th century we had understood that there was a difference between the nature of a single recording, and the nature of the performances of the works recorded on it (see *AACR2*, revised in 1988). Likewise, entity-relationship database models have given rise to an epistemology of the "work," by which we recognize it as a distinct, if abstract, entity. Every instance, physical or sonic, is just an instantiation (Thomas and Smiraglia 1998; Smiraglia 2002a; and *FRBR* [IFLA 1998]).

A second issue was how to represent music in a subject catalog. The answer to this question has been logically answered from the beginning—a subject array for music history, theory, and criticism, and the use of strings utilizing terms for form and medium for the music itself. No other answer could arise because, ontologically speaking, the essence of music is form (including genre) and medium. So over time the argument becomes repetitive: how best to represent these concepts, and in what order are they best presented for retrieval of various sorts. Here at the beginning of the story, in the late 19th century, classificationists are still searching for the one true order of all knowledge. By the end of the 20th century scholars of knowledge organization have declared that a passé idea of the modern period (Mai 1999; Smiraglia 2003), claiming instead that postmodernism demands domain-specific solutions even to problems as simple as this. The revised 780 schedule for the *Dewey Decimal Classification* offers the perfect post-modern solution—a faceted array, to be arranged in domain-specific sequences.

The third major issue, closely related to the second, was how to arrange the music itself for browsing and retrieval. The result was the same, as subjects for history, theory, and criticism, and medium-form combinations for scores, were used as ontologies to underlie classification systems. These concerns were common to librarians working with music in both public and academic libraries, and were to fuel the development of cataloging codes, subject heading lists, and classifications through the next century.

Sound Recordings Complicate Things

We begin in 1887 with the problems of incorporating scores into libraries of books. But shortly after the beginning of the 20th century the introduction of sound recordings into the library created a new set of problems. Ralph Ellsworth's 1933 *Library Journal* article illustrates the introduction of these problems into the developing community of music librarians. The primary problems related to the care and storage of sound recordings, which would remain a rather delicate medium until the computer age. Of course the problems of how to include sound recordings in the catalog and how to arrange them for retrieval predominated as well. Interestingly enough, divergence could be seen between public and academic librarians on the issues of the care and treatment of sound recordings. Academic music librarians were concerned primarily with cataloging and classification of the musical works represented on the recordings. But public librarians were mostly concerned with the arrangement of the recordings for browsing and circulation by the public. This divergence would persist in the literature until the development of the *International Standards for Bibliographic Description (ISBD)* and the *Anglo-American Cataloguing Rules* second edition (*AACR2*) that appeared in the 1970s. To some extent the problem is related to the development of music cataloging practices in divergent discourse communities, and to some extent it is probably an artifact of the scatter of the literature across several such communities. We will return to these issues later in this essay, but the reader should bear in mind the observation made before that difficulty with dissemination of techniques led to repeated revisiting of issues settled in earlier generations (Smiraglia 1989).

The 1940s saw the introduction of printed Library of Congress cards for sound recordings and the beginning of work on catalog codes for music materials. Eva Judd O'Meara's 1941 entry in the American Library Association's *Cataloging & Classification Yearbook* described the development of a music code. This reflects a trend in general librarianship that saw the increasing professionalization of bibliographic control through the twentieth-century based on shared practice and codification. O'Meara's article also stands as one of the rare examples of crossover between the communities of book librarians and music librarians. From the point in 1931 when the Music Library Association formed apart from the American Library Association, until the late 1970s when cooperation on the *Anglo-American Cataloguing Rules* demanded collegiality, the two communities operated apart from each other and mostly unaware of each other's progress.

From the 1930s through the 1950s the literature was flooded with reports of institution-based professional practice. Ranging from "Worcester Free Public Library Gives Discs Full Treatment" (Kemp 1948) to "Classification of Folk Music and Dance . . . for the Cecil Sharp Library" (Dean-Smith 1951) these reports peppered the literature with the experience of librarians who had found successful solutions to the basic problems of descriptive cataloging and arrangement of music materials. The effort was broadly international as well, as we see reports such as the manual for cataloging recordings at the Brazilian national library (Cosme 1949), "Music Cataloguing at the Toronto Public Library" (Page 1945), and an orientation to music cataloging from the Norwegian perspective

(Lellky 1951). Curiously enough, the eleven undated citations in our bibliography all offer works that fall into this category. (See Table 1.)

Table 1: Undated Local Classifications

Brooklyn Public Library
Music literature and scores together, expanded and modified from Dewey 780
Buenos Aires Biblioteca Nacional
Classificación de las obras de musica
Chicago Public Library
Classification for music scores ...
Cleveland Public Library
Music classification
Free Library of Philadelphia
Chamber music classification scheme ...
Greensboro, N.C. Public Schools
Quick reference classification code for non-music records; for music records
Harvard Musical Association Library
Classification of literature; classification of music
Johansson, Corry (Swedish Broadcasting Corporation)
ARAL: A Coordination system of classification
Pittsburgh Public Schools
Outline of classification for recordings ...
Radcliffe College Library
Music classification, literature of music, collections of music; scores of individual composers
Toledo Public Library
Music classification used at Toledo

So rapidly was this literature expanding that Minnie Elmer's 1946 thesis at the Columbia University School of Library Service was an annotated bibliography with a purpose similar to our own—to demonstrate to the community the breadth of the literature that was developing concerning the bibliographic control of music.

Codification, Automation

By the middle of the 20th century, codification was playing a major role. A joint code produced by the Music Library Association (MLA) and the

American Library Association (ALA) appeared in 1958. About the same time (1957) the International Association of Music Libraries (IAML) began to publish its *Code International de Catalogage de la Musique*. A third landmark to appear in this period was the New York Public Library's *Music Subject Headings* compilation, which was published in 1959. Eric Coates' *British Catalog of Music Classification* appeared in this sequence in 1960.

Significant manuals of practice began to appear at this time in rapid succession, including, notably, Eric Bryant's *Music Librarianship: A Practical Guide*, which appeared in 1959. Brian Redfern's *Organizing Music in Libraries* was first published in 1966, representing the first modern monographic treatment of techniques for the bibliographic control of music. Reviews of these landmark texts now began to appear in great numbers as the leading music librarians of the day analyzed these developments and contributed to their international dissemination.

The next major development (which paralleled, of course, general librarianship) was to be automation, and Tanno's 1968 article "Automation and Music Cataloging" was the harbinger of this new front. Not long after, Coover's "Computers, Cataloguing, and Co-operation" (1969) introduced the inter-institutional and international cooperation that was then underway to develop automated catalogs. In 1976 *Music: A MARC Format* was published by the Library of Congress, demonstrating a decade of work on the construction of electronic catalog record formats for music. The format was much too complex for its day, but much of that reflected the desire of music librarians and musicologists to make the best possible use of computers for indexing their very complex collections.

Meanwhile the *Alpha-Numeric System for Classification of Recordings* or *ANSCR* was published in 1969, introducing a potential measure of conformity to public library browsing displays of LP recordings. In academic libraries the revision of rules for descriptive cataloging of music materials was a priority, and criticisms, such as that by Miller (1970), led to efforts to revise the relevant portions of 1967's *Anglo-American Cataloging Rules*. The LP recording had brought a major problem in the cataloging of sound recordings to a head, as academic music librarians sought to fully analyze the musical contents of recordings containing more than one work. Daily's 1975 *Cataloging Phonorecordings* was an important monograph-length treatment of the issues surrounding the difficulty of describing and classifying increasingly large collections of recordings. Revised rules for cataloging recordings appeared in 1976 (*Anglo-American Cataloging Rules: Chapter 14 Revised*). Alongside works by librarians, both public and academic, now began to appear articles from collectors about how to organize private collections of recordings. These pieces appeared in magazines such as *High Fidelity* and *Clavier* and helped to fuel the growth of organizations such as the Association for Recorded Sound Collections (ARSC). International cooperation and development was also taking the foreground in the 1970s as efforts to complete the IAML code informed efforts to extend the ISBD to music and sound recordings. Reports by noted leaders such as the Library of Congress' Fred Bindman (1978) and IAML's Lanzke (1977) reflected this trend. *AACR2* appeared in 1978 with its attempt to unify British and North American practices in one volume. It also contained complex rules for the construction of music uniform titles, ISBD-punctuation (a form of content-designation) with music-specific provisions for description of scores and recordings, and rules for selection of access points that were complex in order to deal with a wide variety of types of sound recordings. Therefrom sprang a wealth of literature, not only the usual reviews but also fervid discussion about the errors in the new code (see, for example, Ravilious 1979). It was only a short time before *AACR2* was revised to correct shortcomings in the new provisions. From 1970 onward the literature expanded at a rapid pace: automated cataloging, discography, OCLC, subject headings, MARC tagging, sound archives, continued international cooperation, and coping with nonwestern musics were major topics of the period. Throughout the period there were also reports on a proposed revision of the music section of the *Dewey Decimal Classification*.

The rise of bibliographic utilities, most notably OCLC (whose formal name changed several times from Ohio College Library Center to the current Online Computer Library Center) meant that libraries all over North America (and later the world) needed professional music catalogers. In the past only libraries that had music departments had required professional music catalogers. But OCLC required that all copy entered meet national standards. This meant that a medium-sized academic library with a music collection now needed a knowledgeable music cataloger to enter records into OCLC. The consequent legions of new music catalogers, graduates of library schools with little or no relevant coursework in music librarianship, gave rise in the 1980s to a new series of manuals for use of *AACR2* and *MARC*. Examples of this genre are Frost (1983), Smiraglia (1983), Weidow (1984), Holzberlein (1988), and Weitz (1990).

Wursten (1983) signaled the beginning of efforts to turn the paper catalogs of the past into the online bibliographic wonders of today. Retrospective conversion was a dream at the beginning of the 1980s but is a dream accomplished today. In between, the literature reflected the massive efforts of librarians worldwide that went into accomplishing this task that had seemed nearly impossible at its inception. Gregor (1984) edited papers from a conference sponsored by the Council on Library Resources—from this conference grew a concerted plan, later called REMUS for Retrospective Conversion of Music, that succeeded in entering a century of cataloging into the bibliographic utilities.

Research and Sophistication

While the literature continued to expand over the 1980s and 1990s, the topics did not really change. What is noticeable is increasing sophistication; more articles in journals and fewer professional reports (about which more later). However, the preponderance of book reviews as a medium of communication remains apparent. As examples of the sophistication of the field, note Schultz (1989) who introduced artificial intelligence technology into the assignment of Dewey numbers, Pavlovsky (1997) on Slavic sacred music, Vellucci (also 1997) on bibliographic relationships, and Colby (1998) on access to 20th century music. Also, Hemmasi (1995 and 1998), working with a group from the Music Library Association, began work on a music thesaurus modeled on the now well-known *Art & Architecture Thesaurus (AAT)*. Finally, the century turns with Krummel's challenge "On Degressive Music Bibliography" (2000) and Papakhian's summary of the century past (2000) "Music Librarianship at the Turn of the Century: Cataloging."

So the sequence is this: The era reported in this literature began with efforts to incorporate music into library catalogs designed for books. There was much gnashing of teeth about how to represent the musical work—this under the guise of how to transcribe titles proper for scores and how to analyze the contents of sound recordings. There was tremendous international cooperation among music librarians that resulted in great professional unity around the world on the solutions to problems of access and retrieval for music materials. A period of trial and error was followed by codification, and the whole effort was fast-forwarded by the introduction of automation and bibliographic utilities and the fulfillment of the promise of shared cataloging. In the end, a century of professionalization of the bibliographic control of music led to increased sophistication in the scholarship brought to bear on these problems.

Some of the problems that emerge from this literature are the divergence of discourse communities. For example, public librarians, academic librarians, music librarians, and archivists were sometimes at odds about techniques. Despite the progress among music librarians in the development of sophisticated techniques for cataloging sound recordings, public librarians seemed unaware or disconnected, perhaps due to a fundamental difference in purpose (retrieval of specific works in the academic world, browsing and circulation in the public library). At the end of the era collectors chimed in, followed by systems librarians well-versed in the capabilities of their computers but often clueless about both music and bibliographic control. We will revisit all of this in the following sections of this essay, but the surprisingly rich demonstration provided by the chronological display of this literature yields an intimate portrait of the development of music cataloging in the past century and a bit.

Our Taxonomy

Subject indexes to the bibliography rely on a taxonomy that was derived from keywords in the titles of the works cited. The purpose of the taxonomy was not to provide depth indexing; rather the purpose was to provide groupings arising from the subjects covered, the better to illustrate the subjects of interest to the authors whose work is represented. Here is the taxonomy arrayed alphabetically:

    academic libraries
    automation
    book reviews
    cataloging rules
    classification
    descriptive cataloging
    descriptive cataloging rules
    discography
    librettos
    MARC
    music librarianship
    musicology
    national libraries
    nonbook materials
    public libraries

retrospective conversion
school libraries
scores
sound recordings
special libraries
subject headings

Here the list is arrayed in tabular form together with the frequencies of occurrence of each term, in descending order:

Table 2: Frequency of Keywords

Keyword	Frequency of Occurrence
descriptive cataloging	350
sound recordings	288
classification	209
scores	153
book reviews	141
subject headings	91
cataloging rules	70
academic libraries	34
automation	34
MARC	31
nonbook materials	30
public libraries	30
music librarianship	25
descriptive cataloging rules	17
retrospective conversion	14
national libraries	13
special libraries	12
musicology	8
librettos	4
discography	3
school libraries	3

The terms were not assigned in mutually exclusive ways, so the frequencies are only indicative (that is, more than one term might be assigned to a particular citation). Still we can see that the main themes from our historical narrative are mirrored here. Descriptive cataloging, classification, and subject headings for scores and recordings are the predominant themes. If we add cataloging rules and descriptive cataloging rules to the number for descriptive cataloging we have 437 citations for works about descriptive cataloging—nearly half of the total.

Academic libraries and public libraries occupy roughly equivalent sectors. Automation, MARC, and retrospective conversion if counted together would yield 79 citations—enough to land the group in the top of the frequency distribution. Clearly this topic came to be of major importance. A very large block of this literature (approximately 16% of the citations) is occupied by book reviews (note that many have no author identified in the source). We will return to this below when we discuss forms of literature, but it is clear for now that the book review has been a major forum for dissemination of new techniques in the bibliographic control of music.

The taxonomy emerged chronologically, evolving along with the broad outlines of the development of the bibliographic control of music. Here is the list arrayed chronologically by the first year of each term's occurrence:

Table 3: Year of First Occurrence of Keyword

Keyword	Date Range
descriptive cataloging	1897
subject headings	1897
public libraries	1901
classification	1902
scores	1902
cataloging rules	1904
music librarianship	1915
descriptive cataloging rules	1920
sound recordings	1933
librettos	1937
academic libraries	1939
book reviews	1939
national libraries	1939
school libraries	1945
nonbook materials	1946
special libraries	1948
musicology	1967
automation	1968
MARC	1968
discography	1979
retrospective conversion	1984

Again it is difficult to make precise statements because the assignment of terms is in some ways subjective. But this distribution demonstrates the evolution of topics over time as we described it in the narrative above.

Discourse Communities and Author Productivity

The term "discourse community" is used in information science to describe groups of scholars who have some degree of interaction with each other around a given set of theoretical assumptions (sometimes referred to as a paradigm). Other terms used similarly, but with slightly different nuance, are "discipline" and "domain." A subtle but important difference is that a discourse community is actively engaged in communication, with ongoing interaction through both formal and informal means. Formal means of interaction, of course, are those we call publication; less formal means are interactions via email, conference attendance, even cocktail chatter at symposia. Sometimes within a discourse community a group of scholars will work together quite closely but behind the scenes. Such a group is called an "invisible college" (see Crane 1969).

Bibliometrics, the use of quantitative methods to investigate processes of written communication, is a field of study within information science by which we seek to understand the interaction in discourse communities. Certain techniques, such as citation analysis and network analysis, can be used to demonstrate membership in and research directions of discourse communities. More complex techniques, such as co-citation analysis and co-word analysis, can be used to demonstrate the evolution of an idea, or even the activity of an individual college. In the latter case the evidence accrues when many authors begin to co-cite authors together, demonstrating a convergence of ideas.

In the present essay we will take only a cursory look at the issue of discourse communities. We should remember that bibliometric techniques are partially qualitative, beginning with the deliberate selection and definition of a group of authors, journals, or subjects, from which citation counts can be extracted. We will not attempt to investigate citations—although we hope this bibliography will provide a base bibliography and that this essay will spur such research. Instead, we will look at very simple totals that we think demonstrate the presence of distinct communities working together across the course of the past century to resolve the problems of the bibliographic control of music. We have already suggested what we hope to demonstrate: that music librarians, academic librarians, public librarians, and sound recording collectors all constituted distinct groups. The question is, to what extent were they working together, and therefore communicating with each other? Also, we have posited a sort of professional paradigm with our three big questions: how to handle musical works, how to provide subject access to music, and how to arrange or classify musical documents (scores and recordings).

Author Productivity

We begin by looking for the most productive authors in our bibliography. Those authors with large numbers of citations represent members of what is sometimes seen as a "research front" in a scientific community. That means they are pressing forward with new innovations, leading the community toward solutions to the problems posed in the common paradigm. We caution the reader to remember that we are working here with simple totals and not with citation counts. (Citations *to* works by prolific authors are the real measure of a research front, because they indicate that a given author's ideas have been accepted and are being promulgated by other scholars.) The following table demonstrates authors in our bibliography whose names appear at least five times:

Table 4: Author Productivity

Author	Frequency	Period	Subject
Cunningham 📖	13	1950-1984	cataloging rules
Bryant 📖	11	1951-1985	sound recordings
Smiraglia 📖	10	1981-1997	descriptive cataloging
Bradley 📖	7	1966-1986	music librarianship
Morner 📖	7	1954-1967	sound recordings
Redfern 📖	7	1966-1991	classification
Stevenson	6	1963-1982	sound recordings
Barnhart	5	1990-2000	book reviews
Elmer	5	1942-1961	music librarianship
Hemmasi 📖	5	1992-2000	subject headings
McColvin 📖	5	1924-1965	music librarianship
Miller, Philip	5	1937-1972	sound recordings
Schiodt	5	1969-1982	automation

📖 Indicates one or more major monographs

The authors are listed in descending order based on the number of citations in the bibliography, and in alphabetical order when the number of citations is equal. (Note, we use the term "productivity" loosely here;

we mean simply the contribution we find in this set of documents. Many other authors in music librarianship are just as productive or even more productive than these.) It is an interesting list, which easily divides itself into three groups: Cunningham, Bryant, and Smiraglia constitute the group of authors with greater than 10 citations, the rest hover around 5 each. (This division is based on a statistical concept called a "Bradford distribution." It simply means that the most productive tend to land in the top segment of the distribution and that the bottom of the distribution [in this case everyone who isn't included in this table] is proportionate to the upper segment. For more on Bradford distributions see Bradford 1948). But for now let us simply examine the contributions of these authors.

Virginia Cunningham's contributions span more than three decades from 1950 to 1984; her topics focus primarily around catalog code development and practices at the Library of Congress. Her major monograph is volume 3 of the IAML international code *Rules for Full Cataloging* (1971). Bryant's contributions span the same period, 1951-1985. Bryant is the author of a text, *Music Librarianship* (1959); most of his other publications have to do with sound recordings. Both Bryant and Cunningham contributed three reviews. Smiraglia's contributions are later and more focused: they range from 1981 to 1997 and are almost exclusively contributions in descriptive cataloging, including two manuals of practice. He also contributed a text, *Music Cataloging* (1989), but no reviews.

Bradley's contributions span the period from 1966 to 1986, and consist of four major monographs—perhaps most notably 1966's *Manual of Music Librarianship* and 1972's *Dickinson Classification*—and three journal articles, of which 2 were about the history of music librarianship. Morner, a Swedish music librarian, contributed papers between 1954 and 1967, most about the classification of sound recordings with one monograph, 1962's *Classifikation*. He also contributed 3 reviews. Redfern's contributions span the period from 1966 to 1991 and consist of six editions of his text *Organizing Music in Libraries* (first ed. 1966), and one journal article about the revised *Dewey* classification for music. Stevenson has six contributions spanning the period from 1963 to 1982, mostly about sound recording collections; these comprise five articles and one review.

Barnhart, Elmer, Hemmasi, McColvin, Miller, and Schiodt each have 5 contributions. Elmer's are perhaps the earliest, ranging from 1942-1961, mostly dealing with music librarianship in a holistic way. Schiodt's include 2 papers (one a review) about the IAML code, and the rest about automation, all published between 1969 and 1982. Philip L. Miller's 5 contributions span a period from 1937 to 1972, most about sound recordings and all but one book reviews. Hemmasi's 5 papers, published between 1992 and 2000, are all about subject headings or the project to create a music thesaurus, and include an edition of Library of Congress music subject headings. McColvin's span the period 1924 to 1965; there are 2 editions of his text *Music Libraries*, the first from 1937, one review of Bryant's text, and 2 early articles about music in public libraries. Finally, Barnhart's 5 contributions are all reviews of books, ranging from 1990-2000.

What we see is a firm and consistent "core" of essential literature, produced by authors who Crane (1969) might call "gatekeepers" because they serve to disseminate the collective wisdom of the group. There are no outsiders in this group; all of them could be called "music librarians" in one way or another. Their contributions are consistent and significant, and they all are working with the three paradigmatic questions. One interesting fact: most of them in the upper tier produced a major monograph. One anomaly: McColvin probably ought to be in the upper tier; this is probably an artifact of our bibliography—meaning we probably have missed some citations of his works.

On the other hand, the cutoff here at 5 is a qualitative judgement, thereby missing such notables as Franz Grasberger and Lenore Coral. Also, we did not count organizations; for instance the Library of Congress is "author" of eight works, and the Music Library Association of six. What we do see is a solid core focused on a set of questions of importance to the whole community. The question of whether these works have had impact or not could be answered only by using citation analysis.

One interesting bibliometric conclusion: our bibliography demonstrates Lotka's Law of author productivity. In brief, Lotka says that roughly 60% of all authors in a given distribution contribute only once. This law holds in many distributions discovered by information scientists—perhaps the most interesting to librarians is Arlene Taylor's (then Dowell) discovery that *AACR2* would not have the impact everyone feared, because most authors only have one entry in the catalog (because they only published one work), and therefore catalogers would not need to retrospectively reformulate name headings for most authors already in the catalog (see Dowell 1982, and Smiraglia 2002b). In our distribution we see Lotka's law at work—59.4% of the names in this list are unique; that is, they have only one citation. It means two things—first, that a small core of authors acting as gatekeepers determine how the parameters of the paradigm are disseminated, and second, and more egalitarian, that a huge number of people have contributed what they know to the furtherance of the paradigm. Music is better controlled now that it was 100 years ago, because of the hard work of these individuals, and because of their contributions to the paradigm.

Author Productivity by Subject

That said, it seems interesting to take a look at the names of authors who are highly productive in different subject areas. In the next table we look only at keywords where authors have more than five publications.

Table 5: Author Productivity by Keyword

Keyword	Prolific author
Book reviews	Barnhart 5
	Whitehead 5
Classification	Redfern 6
	Cunningham 5
Descriptive cataloging	Cunningham 9
	Smiraglia 7
	Elmer 5
	Redfern 5
Music librarianship	Bradley 5
Scores	Smiraglia 5
Sound recordings	Bryant 6
	Smiraglia 5
Subject headings	Hemmasi 5
	Redfern 5

Here we see no surprises; the same authors as before, but with a better sense of the focus of their contributions.

Divergence or Egalitarianism?

Here we want to look at the issue of whether there are different folks contributing information about the same set of three issues from different perspectives. We already have plenty of evidence that this is the case.

From Brown to Papakhian: An Essay

But if we look briefly at the authors whose works are characterized narrowly as "Academic" or "Public" or "Discography," we see that we do, indeed, have distinct groups of contributors. Here is a table of the authors in each group:

Table 6: Authors in Academic, Public and Discography Groups

Academic	Public	Discography
Anderson, Jean	Berkshire Athaneum	Eick
Barnes, Christopher	Brooklyn Public Library	Gray
Benton, Rita	Bryant, Eric Thomas	Griffin
Bixler, Paul Howard and Mills, Julia Louise	Chicago Public Library	
Bull, Cecil	Cleveland Public Library	
California University Library	Deutscher Bibliotheksverband. Arbeitskreis öffentliche Musikbibliotheken. Kommision für Tonträger-Systematik	
Campbell, A. B.	Edmonton Public Library	
Campbell, Freda	Elmer, Minnie	
Chailley, Jacques	Hopkins, J. A.	
Crow, Linda	International Association of Music Libraries. Deutsche Gruppe	
Cundiff, Morgan	Kemp, M. L.	
De Lerma, Dominique-René	Maywhort, Mrs. H. W.	
Devigne, Roger	Millen, Irene	
Foster, Donald L.	Page, A.	
Godfrey, Marlene	Palmer, William W.	
Gorman, Hester	Pearson, Mary D.	
Griffin, Marie	Riddle, C.	
Held, Naomi Edwards	Scholz, Dell DuBose	
Johnson, B. Lamar	Scilken, Marvin H.	
Koth, Michelle and Green, Laura Gayle	Sherlock, M.	
Kranz, Jack	Toledo Public Library	

McGaw, Howard F., comp.	Wassner, H.
Meikleham, M. H. C.	Wegg, M. F.
Milhous, Virginia Alice	
Musiol, Karol	
Radcliffe College Library	
La Roche College, Music Dept.	
Shane, M. Lanning	
Smiraglia, Richard P.	
Stiles, Helen J.	
Thompson, Annie F.	
United States Air Force Academy	
Wienpahl, Robert W.	

There are no names common to these three categories. Both the academic and public lists are international in scope, which is consistent with what we have seen so far. This time we have left the institutional contributors in to demonstrate the degree to which the public library sector has contributed in-house classification systems and operations manuals; this reinforces our sense that the effort to control music has an egalitarian flair to it. On the other hand, the academic library sector and the discography sector consist almost entirely of journal articles (not illustrated here). So there is a distinct difference in the degree of formality brought to bear. Journal publications indicate peer review and wide dissemination of information within a discourse community. Publication of in-house manuals, about a third of the public libraries sector, indicates a less formal system of communication and perhaps a less coherent discourse community.

Scatter of the Literature

Scatter is a bibliometric concept introduced by Bradford that demonstrates the extent to which the literature on a given subject is scattered across different journals or other publication venues. In this essay we will look first at the distinction between journals and other forms of publication, and then we will look at the fascinating importance of book reviews in this subject area. We will see that this literature has even more egalitarian character than we have seen so far—the literature about music cataloging is scattered all over the landscape. Of course, to a scientist or a reference librarian this might present a problem, but it does suggest that the importance of the bibliographic control of music is universal and not limited to a small set of professional librarians.

In this bibliography we have 5 dissertations (or master's theses), 214 monographs or chapters from monographs, and 472 articles in periodicals—54% of the literature is journal literature, 24% is monographic. The journal literature appears in 194 journals or a possible 2.4 articles per journal. That is a distinct measure of scatter. However, if we compile a table of journal titles we see the following:

Table 7: Journal Productivity

Journal	Frequency
Fontes artis musicae	88
Notes	65
Library Journal	41
Library Resources & Technical Services	30
Cataloging & Classification Quarterly	21
Brio	20
Forum Musikbibliothek	15
Library Trends	11
Biblioteksbladet	10
Library Association Record	10
Bogens Verden	9
ARSC Journal	8
High Fidelity	8
Journal of Documentation	8
Library Quarterly	8
College & Research Libraries	7
Library of Congress Information Bulletin	7
Musical Times	7
Notes: Supplement for Members	7
International Cataloguing	6
Journal of Cataloging & Classification	6
Zentralblatt für Bibliothekswesen	6
Bulletin d'Informations de l'Association des Bibliothécaires Français	5

Indexer	5
Library World	5
Recorded Sound	5
ALA Bulletin	4
American Record Guide	4
Australian Library Journal	4
Bollettino d'informazioni (Associazione Italiana Biblioteche)	4
Illinois Libraries	4
Librarian & Book World	4
North Carolina Libraries	4
Pacific Northwest Library Association Quarterly	4
Assistant Librarian	3
Audiovisual Librarian	3
Bibliotekar	3
Bibliothekar	3
Bok og Bibliotek	3
Catalogue & Index	3
Information Technology and Libraries	3
Kirjastolehti	3
Muzyka	3
Nachrichten (Vereinigung Schweizerische Bibliothekare)	3
North Western Newsletter	3
Ontario Library Review	3
Phonographic Bulletin	3
Prezeglad Biblioteczny	3
Special Libraries	3
Technical Services Quarterly	3
Unabashed Librarian	3

Everything else, from *Catholic Library World* to *Zeitschrift für Musikwissenschaft* has fewer than 2 citations. Actually, what we see here is a normal Bradford distribution again—this time we are looking at journal productivity. Typically the cutoff would have been at 5, but I wanted readers to see the breadth of this list. *Fontes, Notes, LRTS, CCQ & Brio* are all peer-reviewed formal journals, and they contain the largest quantity of material. *Library Journal*, on the other hand, is a major venue for communication all across the discipline of librarianship and particularly important for reaching public librarians. Notice also the significant presence of public sector magazines such as *High Fidelity, Stereo Review*, and *Billboard*. *Fontes, Notes,* and *Brio* are all journals of music librarianship, while *LRTS* & *CCQ* are technical services journals. So we have an interesting mix—the formal venues of music librarianship are the principal means of dissemination. However, the focus on problems of cataloging and classification means that the tools of technical services and bibliographic control have been brought to bear as well. We must bear in mind that that means the techniques being vetted by music specialists have received peer approval to be disseminated in these journals. And, ultimately, the public library sector has found its voice as well. The question remains, were these distinct sectors communicating with each other?

Another interesting note on venues is the large number of local and specialized journals—everything from *Ontario Library Review, Pacific Northwest Library Association Quarterly, Illinois Libraries* to *Pakistan Library Review* and *Brussels Museum of Musical Instruments Bulletin*. This is more evidence of the egalitarian nature of the effort to control music, and also of the international scope of the effort. However, it also contributes to the degree of scatter. Thirty percent of the material appears in the top six journals in the distribution; that means that 70% is scattered among the other 168 venues.

On Book Reviews

We have taken note several times of the prominence of book reviews among the works in this bibliography. Often in discourse communities book reviews play a useful but not prominent role. Particularly in communities of scientists, in which the journal or technical report constitute the primary means of communication, books play a less important role in furthering the paradigm. But not in this case. Here we see a community of international scope, with a strong egalitarian character, in which the core of prolific authors seem to be defined by the production of major monographs. Consequently, the book review itself becomes a primary vehicle of communication. These reviews go beyond the mere evaluation of texts and contribute to the international dissemination of techniques for the bibliographic control of music.

For instance, there are nineteen reviews between 1964 and 1972 of Curall's *Gramophone Record Libraries* (1963). Currall contributes only three citations to this bibliography, but clearly the community eagerly received the text and widely disseminated reviews. Another interesting note, is that Linda Barnhart falls into the distribution of prolific contributors at nearly every level—and her entire contribution in this bibliography consists of reviews of important books of the day. It is an interesting illustration of the importance of the gatekeeping role in this discourse community, that authors can reach prominence by passing public judgment on key texts.

Have We Degressed Enough? A Conclusion of a Sort

Krummel (1984) writes that "it is not only possible but very easy for the compiler's work to consist entirely of burrowing. The burrowing becomes seductive, even exciting, when unexpected things turn up." This essay is a perfect example of how one can burrow extensively through the bibliographic history of a discourse community. We have dug into keywords and journal titles and prolific authors and in turn we have demonstrated the remarkable richness of the literature of the bibliographic control of music.

Have we answered our questions? Not entirely. We have demonstrated that the pursuit of the big three questions—works, subjects, and classifications—define the paradigm around which the material included here evolved. We have demonstrated a consistent and evolving core of key authors over time, as demonstrated by the numbers of their contributions and the numbers of reviews of them. We have hinted at both diversity and egalitarianism in the makeup of this discourse community (or of these discourse communities).

We have missed some important highlights. Some of the key literature of music librarianship has not yet been mentioned in this essay. Papers such as Olga Buth's "Scores and Recordings" contribution to a 1974 issue of *Library Trends* had major impact on the position of music librarianship in the panoply of American librarianship. Yet because we have focused on measures of profligacy we have not necessarily defined the key texts of this era.

Krummel has suggested that there is a degressive principle of music bibliography such that a bibliographer might move along a continuum of detail depending on the importance of a given citation (or work) to a specific bibliographic purpose. Certainly the ProCite™file from which this essay is drawn is organized along a degressive principle. We have only as much bibliographical detail as the sources from which these citations were drawn allow us. And for our purpose, which is to study the bibliographic control of music, that is sufficient. But another bibliographer another day might well wish we had hunted down paper copies of all of these works. And certainly better answers to our questions about the divergence of the elements of this discourse community and the scatter of the literature can be better answered by rigorous bibliometric analysis. We hope this bibliography spurs such research.

In the meantime, we think this bibliography stands as a monument to more than a century of effort by music librarians around the world to improve methods for the control of music materials and especially for their retrieval. The prize is the ability of people around the world to interact with the sonic treasures of human creation.

Works Cited

Bindman, Fred. 1978. ISBD (Music) progress reported. *Library of Congress information bulletin* 37: 339.
Bradford, S. C. 1948. *Documentation*. Washington, D.C.: Public Affairs Press.
Bradley, Carol June. 1966. *Manual of music librarianship*. Ann Arbor: Music Library Association.
Bradley, Carol June. 1968. *The Dickinson classification: a cataloging and classification manual for music, including a reprint of the George Sherman Dickinson classification of musical compositions*. Carlisle, Pa.: Carlisle Books.
Bradley, Carol June. 2003. Classifying and cataloging music in American libraries: an historical overview. *Cataloging & classification quarterly* 35n4: 467-81.
Brown, James Duff. 1897. Cataloguing of music. *Library* 9: 82-84.
Bryant, Eric Thomas. 1959. *Music librarianship: a practical guide*. London: James Clarke.
Buth, Olga. 1974. Scores and recordings. *Library trends* 23: 427-50.
Coates, Eric J. 1960. *The British catalogue of music classification*. London: Council of the British National Bibliography.
Colby, Michael D. 1998. Nailing Jell-O to a tree: improving access to 20th-century music. *Cataloging & classification quarterly* 26n3: 31-9.
Coover, James B. 1969. Computers, cataloguing, and co-operation. *Notes* 25: 437-46.

Cosme, Luiz. 1949. *Manual de classifcacao e catalogacao de discos musicais.* Rio de Janeiro: Brazil Institute de Livro, Departamento de imprensa nacional.

Crane, Diana. 1969. *Invisible colleges: diffusion of knowledge in scientific communities.* Chicago: University of Chicago Press.

Curall, Henry F. J. 1963. *Gramophone record libraries: their organization and practice.* London: C. Lockwood.

Cutter, Charles Ammi. 1876. *Rules for a printed dictionary catalog.* Public libraries in the United States of America, part II. Washington, D.C.: Government Printing Office.

Daily, Jay E. 1975. *Cataloging phonorecordings: problems and possibilities.* New York: Marcel Dekker.

Dean-Smith, Margaret. 1951. Classification of folk music and dance (with relevant subjects) prepared for the Cecil Sharp Library. *Journal of documentation* 7: 215-20.

Dowell, Arlene Taylor. 1982. *AACR2 Headings: a five-year projection of their impact on catalogs.* Littleton, Colo.: Libraries Unlimited.

Ellsworth, Ralph E. 1933. Phonograph records in the library. *Library Journal* 58: 529-31.

Elmer, Minnie. 1946. Music cataloging, with an annotated bibliography of useful reference sources. New York: Columbia University, School of Library Service (M. S. thesis).

Frost, Carolyn O. 1983. *Cataloging nonbook materials: problems in theory and practice.* Littleton, Colo.: Libraries Unlimited.

Hemmasi, Harriette. 1995. The music thesaurus project at Rutgers University. *New Jersey libraries* 28n2: 21-23.

Hemmasi, Harriette. 1998. *Music subject headings.* Soldier Creek music series. Lake Crystal, Minn.: Soldier Creek Press.

Holzberlein, Deanne and Jones, Dolly. 1988. *Cataloging sound recordings: a manual with examples.* New York: Haworth Press.

International Association of Music Libraries. 1957-1983. *Code international de catalogage de la musique.* New York: C.F. Peters.

International Federation of Library Associations, Study Group on the Functional Requirements for Bibliographic Records. 1998. *Functional Requirements for Bibliographic Records.* München: K.G. Saur.

Kemp, M. L. 1948. Worcester Free Public Library gives discs full treatment. *Library journal* 73: 406-8.

Krummel, D. W. 1984. *Bibliographies: their aims and methods.* London: Mansell.

Krummel, Donald W. 2000. On degressive music bibliography: music scores may be described and cataloged differently according to historical attributes: revised version of a paper presented at the University of Pennsylvania, May 1999. *Notes* 56: 867-78.

Lanzke, H. 1978. ISBD (Music): first meeting of the IFLA/IAML Working Group in Mainz, 29-21 September 1977. *Fontes artis musicae* 25: 105.

Lellky, Ake. 1951. Katalogisering av musikalier: en orientering. *Nordisk tidskrift for bok-och biblioteksvasen.*

Mai, Jens-Erik. 1999. A postmodern theory of knowledge organization. *Proceedings of the 62nd annual meeting of the American Society for Information Science*, ed. Larry Woods. Medford, N.J.: Information Today, 1999, 547-56.

Miller, Miriam. 1970. AACR 1967, Chapters 13 & 14: a music librarian's view of a cataloging code. *Brio* 7: 27-31.

Music Library Association and the American Library Association, Division of Cataloging and Classification. 1958. *Code for cataloging music and phonorecordings*. Chicago: American Library Association.

New York Public Library. Reference Department. 1959. *Music subject headings authorized for use in the catalogs of the Music Division*. Boston: G.K. Hall.

O'Meara, Eva Judd. 1941. Music code. In American Library Association *Cataloging & Classification Yearbook* 10: 68-69.

Page, A. 1945. Music cataloguing at the Toronto Public Library. *Ontario library review* 29: 161-63.

Papakhian, Arsen Ralph. 2000. Music librarianship at the turn of the century: cataloging. *Notes* 56: 581-90.

Pavlovsky, Taras. 1997. Slavic sacred music: issues in cataloguing: paper presented at the 1997 MLA conference. *Fontes artis musicae* 44: 248-65.

Ravilious, C. P. 1979. AACR2 and its implications for music cataloguing. *Brio* 16: 2-12.

Redfern, Brian L. 1966. *Organizing music in libraries*. London: Clive Bingley.

Saheb-Ettaba, C. and McFarland, R. B. 1969. *ANSCR: the alpha-numeric system for classification of recordings*. Williamsport, Pa.: Bro-Dart.

Schultz, Lois S. 1989. Designing an expert system to assign Dewey classification numbers to scores. *National online meeting proceedings 1989, New York 9-11 May*, ed. C. Padgett and L. Nixon. Medford, N.J.: Learned Information, 393-97.

Smiraglia, Richard P. 1983. *Cataloging music: a manual for use with AACR2*. Lake Crystal, Minn.: Soldier Creek Press.

Smiraglia, Richard P. 1989. *Music cataloging: the bibliographic control of printed and recorded music in libraries.* Littleton, Colo.: Libraries Unlimited.

Smiraglia, Richard P. 2002a. Musical works and information retrieval. *Notes: The quarterly journal of the Music Library Association* 58: 747-64.

Smiraglia, Richard P. 2002b. Further progress in theory in knowledge organization. *Canadian journal of information and library science.* 26n2/3: 30-49.

Smiraglia, Richard P. 2003. The history of "the work" in the modern catalog. *Cataloging & classification quarterly* 35n3/4: 553-67.

Tanno, J. 1968. Automation and music cataloging. *College music symposium* 8: 48-50.

Thomas, David H. and Richard P. Smiraglia. 1998. Beyond the score. *Notes* 54: 649-66.

Vellucci, Sherry L. 1997. *Bibliographic relationships in music catalogs.* Lanham, Md.: Scarecrow.

Weidow, Judy. 1984. *Music cataloging policy in the General Libraries.* Contributions to librarianship. Austin: University of Texas General Libraries.

Weitz, Jay. 1990. *Music coding and tagging.* Soldier Creek music series. Lake Crystal, Minn.: Soldier Creek Press.

Bibliographic Control of Music 1897-2000: A Chronological Listing

Publications issued without date are listed alphabetically at the end.

1. Brown, James Duff. 1897. Cataloguing of music. *Library* 9: 82-84. Variantly cited as "Classification scheme for music libraries" in some bibliographic sources.
2. Discussion on classification of music by members of the Massachusetts Library Club. 1901. *Public Libraries* 6: 639-40.
3. Discussion on the catalogue of the Boston Library. 1902. *Library Journal* 27, no. 190-192.
4. Ayer, Clarence W. 1902. Shelf classification of music. *Library Journal* 27: 5-11.
5. Cutter, Charles Ami. 1902. Shelf classification of music. *Library Journal* 27: 68-72.
6. Library of Congress. 1904. *Class M—Music; Class ML—Literature of music; Class MT—Music instruction.* Washington, D.C.: Library of Congress.
7. Sonneck, Oscar George T. 1904. *Music: rules for a dictionary catalog.* 4th ed., rewritten ed., Charles Ami Cutter, 138-40. Washington, D.C.: U.S. Govt. Printing Office.
8. Hopkins, J. A. 1907. Music in libraries. *Wisconsin Library Bulletin* 3: 89-93.
9. Riddle, C. 1914. Music in public libraries. *Library Association Record* 16: 9-10.
10. Symposium on music in libraries: Contributed by various libraries in the United States. 1915. *Library Journal* 40: 561-94.

11. Kinkeldey, Otto. 1915. American music catalogs. *Library Journal* 40: 574-78.
12. Cataloging of music in the Seattle Public Library. 1917. *American Library Annual* 64.
13. Library of Congress. 1917. *Classification. Class M, Music; Class ML, Literature of music; Class MT, Musical instruction.* Washington, D.C.: Library of Congress. 2d ed. with supplementary pages.
14. Sonneck, Oscar George T. 1917. Prefatory note. *Classification. Class M, Music; Class ML, Literature of music; Class MT, Musical instruction.* 2d ed., with supplementary pages, ed. Library of Congress, 5. Washington, D.C.: For sale by the Card Division, Library of Congress.
15. Report of ALA Committee on Catalog Rules: Rules for cataloging musical scores. 1920. *ALA Bulletin* 14: 295-96.
16. American Library Association. Committee on Catalog Rules. 1920. Rules for cataloging of musical scores. *ALA Bulletin* 14: 295-96.
17. Bishop, William W. 1920. Report of ALA Committee on Catalog Rules: Rules for cataloging musical scores. *ALA Bulletin* 14: 295-96.
18. Cataloging the small music collection. 1924. *Library Journal* 49: 227.
19. McColvin, Lionel R. 1924. *Music in public libraries.* London: Grafton. Chapter 2: Cataloguing; Chapter 3: Classification.
20. Schmidt-Phiseldeck, Kay. 1926. *Musikalienkatalogisierung; ein Beitrag zur Lösung ihrer Probleme.* Leipzig: Breitkopf & Härtel. Translation: The cataloging of printed music: A contribution to the solution of its problems.
21. Wallace, Ruth. 1927. *Care and treatment of music in a library.* Chicago: American Library Association.
22. Pietzsch, Gerhard W. 1929. *Klassifikation der Musik von Boetius bis Ugolino von Orvieto.* Halle: Karras, Korber & Nietschmann. Translation: The classification of music from Boethius to Ugolino of Orvieto.
23. Schneider, C. 1931. Schlagwortkatalog der musikwissen-schaftlichen Literatur auf systematischer Grundlage. *Zeitschrift für Musikwissenschaft* 13: 11-12. Translation: A subject catalog of musicological literature based on systematic foundations.
24. Ohman, Hazel Eleanor. 1932. *Music subject heading system: The outline of an expansive decimal system for a logical classification of musical literature.* New York: Author.

25. Ellsworth, Ralph E. 1933. Phonograph records in the library. *Library Journal* 58: 529-31.
26. Uspenskaa, S. L. 1935. Klassifikatsiia notnoi literatury po tselevomu nazanacheniiu. *Sovetskaia Bibliografia* 1-2: 119-30. Translation derived from abstract: A scheme of classification for musical works.
27. Catalog of music collection. 1937. *Pacific BinderyTalk* 10: 68.
28. Amesbury, Dorothy G. 1937. Phonograph records in the library. *Library Journal* 62: 453-54.
29. Currier, Thomas Franklin. 1937. Librettos. *Library Journal* 62: 794.
30. Devigne, Roger. 1937. Documentation sonore et la phonothèque du Musée de la Parole de l'Université de Paris. *World congress of universal documentation*, 82-84. Paris: Secretariat. Summary in *International Institute of Documentation quarterly communications* 1937 4, no. 4: 28-29. Translation derived from abstract: Sonic documentation and the phonograph library of the language museum at the University of Paris.
31. Hanauer, Julius. 1937. Vorschlag zur Dokumentation über Musik. *World congress of universal documentation*, 169-70. Paris: Secretariat. Translation: A proposal for documentation concerning music.
32. McColvin, Lionel R. 1937. Classification and cataloguing of music in Public Libraries. *Wen-Hua Chi-k'an* 9: 201-8. Translation into Chinese by Chia-chieh Ku.
33. McColvin, Lionel R. and Reeves, Harold. 1937. *Music libraries*. London: Grafton. Chapter 2: Cataloguing; Chapter 3: Classification.
34. Miller, Philip L. 1937. Cataloging and filing of phonograph records. *Library Journal* 62: 544-46.
35. Spivacke, Harold. 1937. The cataloging of folk-song records. *Notes* 5: 9-16.
36. Dickinson, George Sherman. 1938. *Classification of musical compositions: a decimal-symbol system*. Poughkeepsie, N. Y.: Vassar College.
37. Russell, John F. 1938. The cataloguing of music. *Library Association Record* 40: 247-50.
38. Weiss-Reyscher, E. 1938. *Anweisung zur Titelaufnahme von Musikalien*. Leipzig: Einkaufshaus für Büchereien. Translation: Instructions for the descriptive cataloging of printed music.
39. Victrola Records Popular. 1939. *ALA bulletin* 33: 258.
40. Anker, Oyvind. 1939. Katalogisering av Musikalier. *Bok og Bibliotek* 6: 37-43. Translation: The cataloging of music.

41. Heyer, Anna Harriet. 1939. Policies of cataloging and classification in self-contained music libraries. *ALA cataloging & classification yearbook* 8: 126-28.
42. Heyer, Anna Harriet. 1939. "Policies of cataloging and classification in self-contained music libraries." Columbia University. M.S. thesis.
43. McPherson, Harriet D. 1939. The philosophy of classification and of classifying. *Library quarterly* 9: 321-31.
44. O'Meara, Eva Judd. 1939. Review. Dickinson, G. S. *Classification of musical compositions; a decimal-symbol system. Library quarterly* 9: 228-30.
45. Shane, M. Lanning. 1939. Audio-visual aids and the library. *College & research libraries* 1: 143-46.
46. Simons, Fanny. 1939. *Regels voor de Titelbeschrijving en Schema van een systematische Indeeling van Musiekwerken.* 's- Gravenhage: Uitgeversfond der Bibliotheekvereningen. Centrale Vereeniging voor openbare Leeszalen en Bibliotheken Leeszaalwek N.3. Translation: Rules for descriptive cataloging and a scheme of systematic classification for printed music.
47. Code for cataloguing music. 1940. *Notes* 8: 60.
48. Music Library Association. 1940. *Special Libraries* 31: 137.
49. Printed cards for phonograph records. 1940. *Notes* 7: 21-22.
50. *The Selmer music library manual.* 1940. Elkhart, Ind.
51. Columbia Broadcasting System. 1940. *An outline of the disc recordings library of Columbia Broadcasting System.* New York.
52. Music Library Association. 1940. Report: Committee for Cataloging and Filing Phonograph Records. *Notes* 9: 25.
53. American Library Association Catalog Code Revision Committee and [British] Library Association. 1941. *ALA catalog rules: Author and title entries.* Chicago: American Library Association.
54. Bixler, Paul Howard and Mills, Julia Louise 1941. We shall have music. *Library Journal* 66: 16-19.
55. O'Meara, Eva Judd. 1941. Music code. *American Library Association cataloging & classification yearbook* 10: 68-69.
56. Music Library Association. Cataloging Committee. 1941-1942. *Code for cataloging music; preliminary version issued by chapters.* Washington, D.C.: The Association, C. V. Nimitz Public Library.
   Chapter 1: *Music, entry and heading* reprinted from ALA catalog rules preliminary 2nd American ed. Chicago: ALA, 1941.
   Chapter 2: *Title.* 1941.
   Chapter 3: *Imprint.* February 1942.

Chapter 4: *Collation*. 1942.
Chapter 5. *Notes.* 1942.
Code for cataloging phonograph records. 1942.
57. Campbell, Freda. 1942. Music cataloging problems in a university library: abridged. *Pacific Northwest Library Association quarterly* 7: 42-43.
58. Elmer, Minnie. 1942. Music cataloging in a public library; abridged. *Pacific Northwest Library Association quarterly* 7: 40-42.
59. Johnson, B. Lamar. 1943-1944. Audio-visual aids and the college library. *College & research libraries* 5: 341-46.
60. Smith, Sidney Butler. 1944. Simplified procedures for recordings. *Library journal* 69: 211-12.
61. Deutsch, Otto Erich. 1945. Plea for a British union catalogue of old printed music. *Journal of documentation* 1: 41-44.
62. Haskell, Inez. 1945. The cataloging of records, Musical and non-musical, for a general library. *Pacific Northwest Library Association quarterly* 9: 150-55.
63. Meikleham, M. H. C. 1945. Cataloging the record collection in McMaster University Library. *Ontario library review* 29: 154-57.
64. Page, A. 1945. Music cataloguing at the Toronto Public Library. *Ontario library review* 29: 161-63.
65. Pedley, Mrs. K. G. 1945. Serving the school radio station. *School Library Association of California bulletin* 16: 5-6.
66. Sherlock, M. 1945. Cataloguing music and records in the Douglas Library. *Ontario library review* 29: 158-59.
67. Stow, Charles Edward. 1945. Cataloging the non-musical phonograph record. *Library Journal* 70: 20-21.
68. Elmer, Minnie. 1946. "Music cataloging, with an annotated bibliography of useful reference sources." Columbia University School of Library Service. M.S. thesis.
69. Maywhort, Mrs. H. W. 1946. All on the card. Sullivan Memorial Library has record cataloging plan. *Library journal* 71: 806-8.
70. Miller, Catharine K. 1946. Pictures invade the catalog. *Library journal* 71: 804-5.
71. Bush, Helen E. and Haykin, David Judson. 1948. Music subject headings. *Notes* 6: 39-45.
72. Christensen, Inger M. 1948. Must we have that new look in music subject headings? *Library journal* 73: 491.
73. Goldthwaite, Scott. 1948. Classification problems in bibliographies of literature about music. *Library quarterly* 18: 255-63.

74. Kemp, M. L. 1948. Worcester Free Public Library gives discs full treatment. *Library journal* 73: 406-8.
75. Moritz, R. G. 1948. Cataloging phonograph records for the veterans hospitals. *Journal of cataloging & classification* 5: 2-4.
76. Von Oesen, Elaine. 1948. Simple cataloging of audio-visual materials. *Wilson library bulletin* 23: 251-53.
77. Scott, Edith. 1948-1949. Cataloging non-book materials. *Journal of cataloging and classification* 5: 46-47.
78. Cosme, Luiz. 1949. *Manual de classificação e catalogação de discos musicais*. Rio de Janeiro: Brazil Instituto de Livro, Departamento de Imprensa Nacional. Translation: Manual for classification and cataloging of music records.
79. Anderson, Jean. 1950. Auckland University Library. *New Zealand libraries* 13: 257-60.
80. Collison, Robert L. 1950. *The cataloguing, arrangement and filing of serial materials in special libraries*. London: Aslib. [Chap. 5]: Gramaphone records.
81. Cunningham, Virginia A. 1950. Simplified cataloging of music. *Journal of cataloging & classification* 6: 6-7.
82. Schmeider, W. 1950. Zur Katalogisierung der Musica Practica. *Zentralblatt für Bibliothekswesen* 64: 343-51. Translation: On the cataloging of Musica practica.
83. Tracey, Hugh. 1950. *African music research transcription library of gramaphone records: Handbook for librarians*. Johannesburg: Gallo.
84. Van Patten, Nathan. 1950. Some problems in the cataloging of musical manuscripts and printed scores. *Notes: Supplement for members* 12: 5-9.
85. Review. Collison, Robert L. *The cataloguing, arrangement and filing of special materials in special libraries*. 1951. *Notes* 8: 356-7.
86. Bryant, Eric Thomas. 1951. Gramophone record catalogues. *Librarian & book world* 40: 55-59.
87. ———. 1951. Pianoforte music and the decimal classification. *Librarian & book world* 40: 217-18.
88. Dean-Smith, Margaret. 1951. Classification of folk music and dance (with relevant subjects) prepared for the Cecil Sharp Library. *Journal of documentation* 7: 215-20.
89. Dunkin, Paul S. 1951. Petty codes and pedagogues. *Journal of cataloging & classification* 7: 53-57.
90. Ferand, E. T. 1951. Sodaine and unexpected music in the renaissance. *Musical quarterly* 37: 10-27.

Chronological Listing 37

91. Lellky, Ake. 1951. Katalogisering av Musikalier. En Orientering. *Nordisk Tidskrift for Bok-och Biblioteksvasen* 38, no. 2: 75-79. Translation: Cataloging music: an orientation.
92. Look, Wallace C. 1951. "Classification and cataloging of music scores in libraries." University of Chicago. M.A. thesis.
93. Meyer-Baer, Kathi. 1951. Classification in American music libraries. *Music review* 12: 76-82.
94. Music Library Association. Committee on Classification. 1951. Proposed alternate scheme for Dewey M780. *Notes: Supplement for members* 17: 5-15.
95. Music Library Association. Committee on Classification. 1951. Music classification. *Notes. Supplement for members* 15: 9-15.
96. Rovelstad, Betsy. 1951. Music cataloging in the Copyright Office. *Notes* 8: 283-89.
97. Wegg, M. F. 1951. "Manual for the descriptive cataloging of music in the Denver Public Library." University of Denver. A.M. thesis.
98. Conrad's record index. 1952. *Record collector* 7: 263.
99. United States Army Military Band Library. 1952. *Musicana* 26: 16-17.
100. Brown, G. D. 1952. Have you a catalogue of your music library? *Music teacher & piano student* 31: 138 & ff; 188 & ff.
101. Cunningham, Virginia A. 1952. Simplified rules of cataloging of music. *Notes: Supplement for members* 21: 8-10.
102. Dean-Smith, Margaret. 1952. Proposals towards the cataloguing of gramophone records in a library of national scope. *Journal of documentation* 8: 141-56.
103. ———. 1952. Review. Cosme, Luis. *Manual de classificação e catalogação de discos musicais. Journal of documentation* 8: 186-88. Translation: Manual for classification and cataloging of music records.
104. Duncan, Barbara. 1952. Review. Library of Congress. *Music subject headings used on printed catalog cards of the Library of Congress. Notes* 9: 607.
105. Gnarro, B. 1952. Perpetual inventory key to efficient record system. *Billboard* 64: 84.
106. Grasberger, Franz. 1952. Einordnung im Autorenkatalog der Musikdrücke. *Zentralblatt für Bibliothekswesen* 66: 28-47. Translation: The arrangement of printed music in the author catalog.

107. ———. Grasberger, Franz. 1952. Zur Bibliographie und Katalogisierung der Textbücher. *Zentralblatt für Bibliothekswesen* 66: 206-19. Translation: On the bibliography and cataloging of libretti.
108. Howe, J. 1952. Records at your fingertips. *Educational music magazine* 31: 31+.
109. Kenton, Egon F. 1952. A note on the classification of sixteenth-century music. *Musical quarterly* 38: 202-14.
110. Library of Congress. Subject Cataloging Division. 1952. *Music subject headings used on printed catalog cards of the Library of Congress.* Washington, D.C.: U.S. Govt. Printing Office.
111. Line, Maurice B. 1952. A classified catalogue of musical scores: some problems. *Library Association record* 54: 362-64.
112. Milhous, Virginia Alice. 1952. "Music in the catalog department of a small college library." Drexel Institute of Technology. M. L. S. thesis.
113. Stanfield, Mary E. 1952. "Classification of music." Western Reserve University. M. S. L .S. thesis.
114. Towsend, Stella R. 1952. Cataloging of phonograph records. *North Carolina libraries* 10: 38-39.
115. Welcome, Jennie. 1952. Pass the platters, please. *Library journal* 77: 2117-20.
116. Angell, Richard S. 1952-1953. Printed cards for phonorecords: subject headings. *Notes* 10: 198-200.
117. Review. *Rules for descriptive cataloging in the Library of Congress: Phonorecords.* 1953. *Journal of research in music education* 1: 74-75.
118. Review. *Rules for descriptive cataloging in the Library of Congress: Phonorecords.* 1953. *Notes* 10: 631-34.
119. Coopersmith, Jacob Maurice. 1953. Phonorecords. *Library of Congress information bulletin* 12: 2-3.
120. Cunningham, Virginia A. 1953. Heart of the music library. *Music journal* 11: 54-57.
121. Hensel, Evelyn M. 1953. Treatment of nonbook materials. *Library trends* 2: 187-98.
122. Hill, Richard. S. 1953. Some pros and cons regarding an international code for cataloging practical music. *International Association of Music Libraries, Troisième Congrès International des Bibliothéques Musicales Paris*, 37-45 Kassel: Bärenreiter.

123. Jacobson, G. H. 1953. "Methodology of music theory: A typology of the methods of investigation, classification, and arrangement of musical materials." Cited in *Dissertation abstracts* 13.
124. Morsch, Lucille M. et al. 1953. Printed cards for phonorecords. *Notes* 10: 197-98.
125. Rosa Tola de Schwalb, C. 1953. Catalogación y clasificación de musica. *Fenix* 9: 217-33. Translation: The cataloging and classification of music.
126. Schnapper, Edith G. 1953. Union catalogue of old music. *Journal of documentation* 9: 117-21.
127. Vaughn, Evelyn L. 1953. Cataloging recordings in the Illinois State Library. *Illinois libraries* 35: 79-85.
128. A card index for your records. 1954. *Hi-fi music at home* 1: 46.
129. Dehennin, W. 1954. Proeve tot het opstellen van een titelbeschrijving voor oude muziekhandschriften. *Bibliotheekgids* 30: 91-100. Translation: Suggested method of cataloging old music manuscripts.
130. Eustis, Edwina. 1954. Classification of music: Analyzing and classifying music for hospital repertoire and general rules for using it. *Music therapy* 3: 49-55.
131. Herrick, M. D. 1954. Subject and technical specialists' cooperation on a score cataloging project. *Journal of cataloging & classification* 10: 84-86.
132. Hess, Albert G. 1954. The cataloging of music in the visual arts. *Notes* 11: 527-42.
133. Merrill, William S. 1954. *Code for classifiers*. Chicago: American Library Association.
134. Morner, Carl Gabriel Stellen. 1954. Katalogisering av Grammofonskivor. *Biblioteksbladet* 39: 285-93. Translation: Cataloging phonograph records.
135. Olding, R. K. 1954. A System of classification for music and related material. *Australian library journal* 3: 13-18.
136. *Manual for the classification and cataloging of music scores*. 1955. New York: Columbia Univ. (The Vassar-Columbia classification scheme integrated with the cataloging procedure manual of the Columbia University Music Library.)
137. *Manual for the classification and cataloging of music scores: The Vassar-Columbia Classification Scheme integrated with the Cataloging Procedure manual of the Columbia University Music Library*. 1955. New York: Columbia University Music Library. Revised by Virginia G. Haft.

138. Bull, Cecil. 1955. Music scores at the University of Montana. *Journal of cataloging & classification* 11: 39-43.
139. Collison, Robert L. 1955. *The treatment of special material in libraries*. London: Aslib.
140. Duckles, Vincent. 1955. Musical scores and recordings. *Library trends* 4: 164-73.
141. Gee, Mable W. 1955. Sink or swim! *Wilson library bulletin* 29: 381-82.
142. Lincoln, Sister Mary Edmund. 1955. Techniques for handling phonograph records. *Catholic library world* 27: 107-10+.
143. Merlingen, W. 1955. Versuche mit einigen neuen Katalogisierungsgrundsätzen. *Zentralblatt für Bibliothekswesen* 69: 431-48. Translation: Experiments with some new principles of cataloging.
144. Conrad's record index. 1956. *Record collector*: 263.
145. Clough, F. F. and Cuming, G. 1956. Problems of an international gramophone record catalogue. *Fontes artis musicae* 3: 95-108.
146. Lundevall, A. 1956. Katalogisering av Musikalier i Folkbiblioteken. *Biblioteksbladet* 41: 715-19. Translation: Cataloging of printed music in a public library.
147. Olsson, K. 1956. Samarbete efterylses! *Biblioteksbladet* 41: 537. Translation: Cooperation requested!
148. Reinhold, H. 1956. Aufbau und Verwendungsmöglichkeiten einer Discothek wertvoller Gesangsaufnahmen im Sendebetrieb. *Fontes artis musicae* 3: 148-51. Translation: Organization and possible use of a record library of valuable vocal records in a radio station.
149. Schmidt-Phiseldeck, Kay. 1956. The Music Cataloguing Committee at Brussels (IAML). *Fontes artis musicae* 3: 31-32.
150. Schonberg, H. C. 1956. A half-million records (BBC Gramophone Library of Commercial Records). *High fidelity* 6: 62-3+.
151. Quinly, William J. 1956-1957. Audio-visual materials in the library. *Library trends* 5: 294-300.
152. Spear, Jack B. 1956-1957. Films and sound records. *Library trends* 5: 406-16.
153. Record cataloguing. 1957. *High fidelity* 7: 17.
154. Angell, Richard S. 1957. Review. International Association of Music Libraries. *Code international de catalogage de la musique*. *Notes* 15: 110-11.
155. *The humanities and the library: problems in the interpretation, evaluation and use of library materials*. 1957. Chicago: American Library Association.

Chronological Listing 41

156. Berger, Arthur. 1957. A census every month (*Schwann catalog*). *High fidelity* 7: 38-40+.
157. Blom, Eric. 1957. Lexicographer's dilemma: (names with prefixes). *Musical times* 98: 546-47.
158. Brooklyn Public Library. 1957. *Classification scheme: long playing records*. Brooklyn.
159. Davies, J. H. 1957. Review. *Vassar-Columbia classification system and manual. Journal of documentation* 13: 88-89.
160. Elmer, Minnie. 1957. Classification, cataloging, indexing. *Notes: Supplement for members*, no. 25: 23-28.
161. Grasberger, Franz. 1957. *Autoren-Katalog der Musikdrücke*. Frankfurt; New York: C.F. Peters. Der Autoren-Katalog der Musikdrücke = The author catalog of published music; Translation by Virginia A. Cunningham; Code international de catalogage de la musique v. 1
162. Hawthorne, Mrs. G. S. 1957. Library for organists. *Library resources & technical services* 1: 50-51.
163. Helmick, C. 1957. Record cataloguing. *High fidelity* 7: 21-24.
164. Humman, Frances. 1957. Bibliographic control of audio-visual materials: Report of a special committee. *Library resources & technical services* 1: 180-88.
165. King, Alexander Hyatt. 1957. Musical information services of the British Museum. *Journal of documentation* 13: 1-12.
166. Kohler, K. H. 1957. Grundzüge einen analytischen Systems der Sachkatalogisierung der "Musica Practica." *Zentralblatt für Bibliothekswesen* 71: 267-80. Translation: Principles of an analytic system for the subject cataloging of "Musica Practica."
167. Lecompte, Yves. 1957. Comment nous utilisons l'electromécanographie. *Fontes artis musicae* 4: 18-24. Translation: How we use electro-mechanography.
168. Munro, Thomas. 1957. Four hundred arts and types of art: A classified list. *Journal of aesthetics and art criticism* 16: 44-64.
169. Peck, John G. 1957. "Music schedules of the decimal classification: A historical and critical study." University of North Carolina. M. S. L. S. thesis.
170. Robinson, S. A. 1957. "Cataloging of music and records." Western Reserve University. M. S. L. S thesis.
171. Schmidt-Phiseldeck, Kay. 1957. Code international de catalogage. *Fontes artis musicae* 4: 26.
172. Stein, Jay W. 1957. *Command performances: Phonorecords related to books and classified*. Memphis: Southwestern College.

173. International Association of Music Libraries. 1957-1983. *Code international de catalogage de la musique*. New York; Frankfurt: C.F. Peters.
    v.1. Grasberger, Franz. *Der Autoren-Katalog der Musikdrücke*. 1957.
    v.2. Fédoroff, Yvette. *Code restreint*. 1961.
    v.3. Cunningham, Virginia. *Rules for full cataloging*. 1971.
    v.4. Martinez-Göllner, Marie Louise. *Rules for cataloging music manuscripts*. 1975.
    v.5. Wallon, Simone and Dorfmüller, Kurt. *Le catalogage des enregistrements sonores*. 1983.
174. The Cecil Sharp Library: The story of the library, its contents, services, and classification scheme. 1958. London: English Folk Dance and Song Society. Library leaflet, no. 3.
175. Dewey, Harry. 1958. Music and phonorecord code criticized. *Library journal* 83: 1665-68.
176. Hart, Richard and Burnette, Frances. 1958. Non-musical collections. *Library journal* 83: 536-43.
177. Hingorani, Rattan P. 1958. Indian music: Expasion [sic] therefore of D. C. schedules. *Student librarian* 2: 35-40.
178. Hoboken, A. van. 1958. Probleme der musikbibliographischen Terminologie. *Fontes artis musicae* 5: 6-15. Translation: Problems of music-bibliographic terminology.
179. Kingsbury, Raphaella. 1958. "A study of the problems involved in the classification and arrangement of college record collections." Humboldt State College. M. A. thesis.
180. Klein, Arthur Luce. 1958. The spoken recordings: An innovation. *Library journal* 83: 533-35.
181. Mason, Donald. 1958. *A primer of non-book materials in libraries*. London: Association of Assistant Librarians. With an appendix on sound recordings by Jean C. Cowan.
182. McPherson, Beryl and Berneking, Carolyn. 1958. Phonorecord cataloging: methods and practices. *Library journal* 83: 2623-24, 2661-62.
183. Music Library Association and the American Library Association, Division of Cataloging and Classification. 1958. *Code for cataloging music and phonorecordings*. Chicago: American Library Association.

Chronological Listing 43

184. Schmidt-Phiseldeck, Kay. 1958. Internationale Kommission für Katalogisierung von Musikalien. *Fontes artis musicae* 5: 15-20. Translation: International Commission for the cataloging of printed music.
185. Records to enrich the teaching of languages. 1959. *Library journal* 84: 1651-53.
186. *Regeln zur Katalogisierung in der Deutschen Bücherei eingehenden Musikalien.* 1959. Leipzig. Translation: Rules for the cataloging of printed music acquired by the East German National Library.
187. Review. International Association of Music Libraries. *Code international de catalogage de la musique.* 1959. *Journal of research in music education* 7: 157-8.
188. Anderson, Sherman. 1959. Cataloging of "folk music" on records. *Library resources & technical services* 3: 64-65.
189. Berkshire Athenaeum. 1959. *Music classification.* Pittsfield, Mass.: Berkshire Athenaeum.
190. Bridgman, Nanie. 1959. Le classement par incipit musicaux. *Bulletin d'informations de l'Association des Bibliothécaires Français* 4: 301-8. Translation: Arrangement of entries according to musical incipit: History of a catalog.
191. Bryant, Eric Thomas. 1959. *Music librarianship: A practical guide.* London; [New York]: James Clarke; Hafner Pub. Co.
192. Coover, James B. 1959. Review. MLA and ALA. *Code for cataloging music and phonorecords. Library quarterly* 29: 143.
193. Cunningham, Virginia A. 1959. Review. *Regeln zur Katalogisierung in der Deutschen Bücherei eingehenden Musikalien. Notes* 16: 567. Translation: Rules for the cataloging of printed music acquired by the East German National Library.
194. McColvin, Lionel R. 1959. Review. Bryant, Eric Thomas. *Music librarianship: A practical guide. Librarian & book world* 48: 163-64.
195. McMullen, H. T. 1959. Order out of chaos. *High fidelity* 6: 26+.
196. New York Public Library. Reference Department. 1959. *Music subject headings authorized for use in the catalogs of the music division.* Boston: G. K. Hall.
197. Somerville, Sheila A. 1959. Cataloguing of gramophone records. *Librarian & book world*: 97-99.
198. Spalding, C. Sumner. 1959. Review. MLA and ALA. *Code for cataloging music and phonorecords. Library resources & technical services* 3: 230-31.

199. Stajic, Branka. 1959. Review. *Regeln zur Katalogisierung in der Deutschen Bücherei eingehenden Musikalien. Zvuk* 31-32: 83-84. Translation: Rules for the cataloging of printed music acquired by the East German National Library.
200. Tschierpe, Rudolph. 1959. Auxiliary catalogues in the music library. *Fontes artis musicae* 6: 7-9.
201. Millen, Irene. 1959-1960. Patterns of growth in public music libraries. *Library trends* 8: 547-55.
202. Cataloging of records. 1960. *Library journal* 85: 4523-25.
203. Review. Bryant, Eric Thomas. *Music librarianship: A practical guide.* 1960. *Library world* 61: 213-15.
204. Anderson, K. H. 1960. Review. Bryant, Eric Thomas. *Music librarianship: A practical guide. Library Association record* 62: 135.
205. Benton, Rita. 1960. Review. Bryant, Eric Thomas *Music librarianship: A practical guide. Notes* 17: 397-98.
206. Borduas, Jean R. 1960. Simplify record classification. *Library journal* 85: 4244.
207. Briggs, Geoffrey Hugh. 1960. Review. Bryant, Eric Thomas. *Music librarianship: A practical guide. New Zealand libraries* 23: 145-46.
208. Broadhurst, T. S. 1960. Review. Bryant, Eric Thomas. *Music librarianship: A practical guide. North western newsletter* 60: 6.
209. Coates, Eric J. 1960. *The British catalogue of music classification.* London: Council of the British National Bibliography.
210. Cox, C. T. 1960. Cataloging of records. *Library journal* 85: 4523-25.
211. ———. 1960. Cataloging of records. *Junior libraries* 7: 19-21.
212. Cunningham, Virginia A. 1960. Review. Coates, E. J. *The British catalogue of music classification. Notes* 17: 556-57.
213. Cunnion, Theodore. 1960. Cataloging and classification of phonograph records. *Proceedings of the 36th annual Catholic Library Association Conference*: 180-85.
214. Davis, D. K. 1960. Record collections. *Library journal* 85: 3375, 4244.
215. Dougherty, K. 1960. Review. Bryant, Eric Thomas. *Music librarianship: A practical guide. Library journal* 85: 1413.
216. Duck, L. W. 1960. Review. Bryant, Eric Thomas. *Music librarianship: A practical guide. Assistant librarian* 53: 171.
217. ———. 1960. Review. Coates, E. J. *The British catalogue of music classification. Assistant librarian* 53: 172.

Chronological Listing 45

218. Elmer, Minnie. 1960. The music catalog as a reference tool. *Library trends* 8: 529-38.
219. Hallowell, Jared R. 1960. "Some information on the cataloging of phonograph records." University of Michigan. A. M. L. S. thesis.
220. Kohler, K. H. 1960. Zur Problematik der Schallplattenkatalogisierung: Gedanken über ein bibliothekarisches Spezifikum. *Zentralblatt für Bibliothekswesen* 74: 102-6. Translation: On the problems of cataloging records: Thoughts on special library material.
221. Linden, Albert van der. 1960. Classement d'une bibliothèque musicale par F.-J. Fétis. *Revue belge de musicologie* 14: 81-86. Translation: Classification of a musical library by F. J. Fétis.
222. Nettl, Bruno. 1960. "Library classification of music: description and critique of selected systems." University of Michigan. A. M. L. S. thesis.
223. Schaal, Richard. 1960. Review. International Association of Music Libraries. *Code international de catalogage de la musique*. *Musikforschung* 13: 246.
224. Tilin, Marian. 1960. Treat records like books. *Junior libraries* 7: 14-17.
225. ———. 1960. Treat records like books. *Library journal* 85: 4518-21.
226. Watkins, T. T. 1960. Review. Bryant, Eric Thomas. *Music librarianship: A practical guide*. *College & research libraries* 21: 423-24.
227. *Music, libraries and instruments: Papers read at the joint congress, Cambridge, 1959, of the International Association of Music Libraries and the Galpin Society*. 1961. London; New York: Hinrichsen.
228. Bryant, Eric Thomas. 1961. Indexing gramophone records. *Indexer* 2: 90-94.
229. Cunningham, Virginia A. 1961. International code for cataloging music. *Notes* 18: 559-62.
230. ———. 1961. Shelflisting music. *Notes: Supplement for members*, no. 31: 11-13.
231. Duckles, Vincent. 1961. The Washington Library Institute (international code for cataloging music). *Notes* 18: 559+.
232. Elmer, Minnie. 1961. Notes on catalogs and cataloging in some major music libraries of Moscow and Leningrad. *Notes* 18: 545-57.
233. Fédoroff, Yvette. 1961. *Code restreint*. Frankfurt; New York: C.F. Peters. Limited code = Kurzgefasste Anleitung: Code international de catalogage de la musique v. 2

234. Lebeau, E. 1961. Review. *The British catalogue of music classification*. *Bulletin de documentation bibliographique* 6: 489-92.
235. Musiol, Karol. 1961. Organizacja i inwentaryzacja zbiorow muzycznych. *Przeglad Biblioteczny* 29: 281-92. Translation: The organization and inventories of music collections.
236. Pethes, Ivan. 1961. A zenemuvek cimleirasanak nemzetkozi szabalyzata. *Magyar konyvszemle* 77: 335-37.
237. Plesske, Hans-Martin. 1961. Zur Systematik der Musikbibliographien der Deutschen Bücherei. *Fontes artis musicae* 8: 7-20. Translation: On the taxonomy of the music bibliographies of the East German National Library.
238. Smolian, Steve. 1961. Da capo. *American record guide* 27: 512-15.
239. Spivacke, Harold. 1961. Review. Bryant, Eric Thomas. *Music librarianship: A practical guide*. *Library quarterly* 31: 283-84.
240. Cuming, Geoffrey. 1961-1962. Problems of record cataloguing. *Recorded sound* 1: 116-22.
241. Nolan, John L. 1961-1962. Audio-visual materials. *Library trends* 10: 261-72.
242. Plumb, P. and Howard, G., comps. 1961. Abstracts (of some recent articles on gramophone record libraries). *Recorded sound* 1: 164-65.
243. Review. Federoff, Y., ed. 1962. *Code restraint*. *Notes* 19: 247-49.
244. Review. International Association of Music Libraries. 1962. *Code international de catalogage de la musique*. *Studia musicologica* 2: 357-8.
245. Aswegen-Badenhorst, J. G. van. 1962. 'n Praktiese Benadering van die Katalogisering van plate in 'n Onderwyskollegediskoteek. *South African libraries* 29: 97-100. Translation: A practical approach to the cataloging of records in a teachers' college record library.
246. Bryant, Eric Thomas. 1962. *Collecting gramophone records*. London: Focal Press.
247. Bryant, Eric Thomas. 1962. Review. International Association of Music Libraries. *Code international de catalogage de la musique*. *Libri* 12, no. 2: 169-71.
248. Chailley, Jacques. 1962. Catalogage des documents ethnomusicologiques sonores (disques et bandes) de l'Institute de Musicologie de Paris. *Fontes artis musicae* 9: 76-78. Translation: Cataloging of ethnomusicological audio material (records and tapes) of the Paris Institute of Musicology.
249. Cohen, Allen. 1962. Classification of four track tapes. *Library resources & technical services* 6: 360-61.

250. Duck, L. W. 1962. Review. Bryant, Eric Thomas. *Collecting gramophone records. North western newsletter* 73: 8.
251. Eckersley, T. 1962. The recorded programmes libraries of the BBC. *Recorded sound* 1: 184-5.
252. Foster, Donald L. 1962. *Notes used on music and phonorecord catalog cards.* Urbana-Champaign: University of Illinois Library. Occasional papers no. 66.
253. Grasberger, Franz. 1962. Review. International Association of Music Libraries. *Code international de catalogage de la musique. Biblos* 11, no. 2: 106-7.
254. International Association of Music Libraries. Landesgruppe Deutsche Demokratische Republik. 1962. *Regeln für die alphabetische Katalogisierung der Musikalien.* Leipzig: Kommission für Musikalienkatalogisierung.
255. Miller, Philip L. 1962. Review. International Association of Music Libraries. *Code international de catalogage de la musique. Library journal* 87: 746-747.
256. Morner, Carl Gabriel Stellen. 1962. *Grund laggande katalogregler for svenska diskotek.* Lund: Bibliotekstjanst.
257. ———. 1962. *Klassifikation av Grammofon—och Bandupptagninger; Reviderad och Detaljerad Uppstallning av Klassifikationssystemets Avdelning Y.* Biblioteksjanst. Translation: Classification of records and tape recordings. Revised and detailed list of section Y of the classification system.
258. ———. 1962. Review. International Association of Music Libraries. *Code international de catalogage de la musique. Biblioteksbladet* 47: 337.
259. Pilton, J. W. 1962. The phonograph record collection. Part 2: Technical notes. *Edmonton [Canada] Public Library news notes* 7: 1-7.
260. Prokopowicz, Maria. 1962. Katalogowanie Plyt. *Przeglad Biblioteczny* 30: 245-53.
261. Schmeider, W. 1962. Review. International Association of Music Libraries. *Code international de catalogage de la musique. Zeitschrift für Bibliothekswesen und Bibliographie* 9, no. 2: 177-83.
262. Vellekoop, G. 1962. Naar eenheid in het catalogiseren van muziekwerken. *Mens en melodie* 17: 332-33. Translation: Toward unity in the cataloging of musical works.
263. Winkel, E. 1962. Review. International Association of Music Libraries. *Code international de catalogage de la musique. Bogens verden* 44: 125.

264. Zielinska, Bozena. 1962. Wskazowki opracowania plyr gramofonwych w zaresie nagren niemuzycznych. *Bibliotekarz* 29: 239-46. Translation: Suggestions for the cataloging of recordings.
265. Review. Currall, H. F. *Gramophone record libraries: Their organization and practice.* 1963. *Nachrichten (Vereinigung schweizerische Bibliothekare)* 39, no. 6: 192.
266. *Musikkbiblioteket: hjelpebok for bibliotekarer.* 1963. Edited by Ella Arntsen. Oslo: Statens bibliotektilsyn. Translation: The music library: Guidebook for librarians.
267. Bryant, Eric Thomas. 1963. Review. Currall, H. F. *Gramophone record libraries: Their organization and practice. Library world* 65: 220+.
268. ———. 1963. Review. Pearson, Mary D. *Recordings in the public library. Library Association record* 65: 393-94.
269. Burkett, Jack and Morgan, T. S. 1963. *Special materials in the library.* London: Library Association. 14 lectures held at the Library Association and Aslib headquarters: January 17th to April 11th, 1962.
270. California University Library. 1963. *C.U. classification for phonorecords.* Berkeley: University of California Library.
271. Cazeaux, Isabelle. 1963. Review. International Association of Music Libraries. *Code international de catalogage de la musique. Fontes artis musicae* 10: 20-29.
272. Critchley, W. E. G. 1963. Review. Currall, H. F. *Gramophone record libraries: Their organization and practice. Scottish Library Association news* 60: 14-15.
273. Currall, Henry F. J. 1963. *Gramophone record libraries: Their organization and practice.* London: C. Lockwood. At head of title: The International Association of Music Libraries, United Kingdom Branch.
274. Gottwald, C. 1963. Empfehlungen für eine zeitgemässe Katalogisierung von Musikhandschriften. *Zur Katalogisierung mittelalterlicher und neuerer Handschriften.* C. Kottelwesch, 155-69. Frankfurt am Main: Klostermann.
275. Harris, K. G. E. 1963. Review. Currall, H. F. *Gramophone record libraries: Their organization and practice. Assistant librarian* 56: 237-38.
276. International Association of Music Libraries. Deutsche Gruppe. 1963. *Systematik der Musikliteratur und der Musikalien für öffentliche Musikbüchereien.* Reuttingen: Bücherei und Bildung.

Chronological Listing 49

277. International Conference on Cataloguing Principles (1961: Paris). 1963. *Report International Conference on Cataloguing Principles, Paris, 9th-18th October 1961.* London: Organizing Committee of the Conference.
278. Kossman, F. K. H. 1963. Review. International Association of Music Libraries. *Code international de catalogage de la musique. Bibliotheeksleven* 48: 83-84.
279. Lapique Becali, Zoila. 1963. *Catalogación y classificación de la musica cubana.* Habana: Biblioteca National José Martí.
280. Leavitt, D. L. 1963. Review. Currall, H. F. *Gramophone record libraries: Their organization and practice. Notes* 20: 648-50.
281. Line, Maurice B. 1963. Classification for music scores on historical principles. *Libri* 12: 352-63.
282. Miller, Philip L. 1963. Review. Pearson, Mary D. *Recordings in the public library. Library journal* 88: 3056+.
283. Morner, Carl Gabriel Stellen. 1963. Review. Currall, H. F. *Gramophone record libraries: Their organization and practice. Tidskrift för dokumentation* 19, no. 4: 61.
284. Palmer, William W. 1963. "Study of the music at the Toronto Public Library." University of Chicago. M. A. thesis.
285. Pearson, Mary D. 1963. *Recordings in the public library.* Chicago: American Library Association.
286. Plumb, P. 1963. Review. Bryant, Eric Thomas. *Collecting gramophone records. Library world* 64: 252-53.
287. Rovelstad, Betsy. 1963. Condensation of the Library of Congress classification schedule. *Notes: Supplement for members* 34: 1-34.
288. Stevenson, Gordon. 1963. Classification chaos. *Library journal* 88: 3789-94.
289. Stevenson, W. B. 1963. Review. Bryant, Eric Thomas. *Collecting gramophone records. Library Association record* 65: 67.
290. Swain, Olive. 1963. *Notes used on catalog cards.* Chicago: ALA.
291. Review. Currall, H. F. *Gramophone record libraries: Their organization and practice.* 1964. *Brio* 1: 22.
292. Review. Currall, H. F. *Gramophone record libraries: Their organization and practice.* 1964. *Recorded sound* 13: 191-92.
293. Arntsen, Ella. 1964. Review. Currall, H. F. *Gramophone record libraries: Their organization and practice. Reol: nordisk bibliotekstidsskrift* 3: 49.
294. Barnes, Christopher. 1964. Review. Currall, H. F. *Gramophone record libraries: Their organization and practice. College & research libraries* 25: 231-32.

295. Brandt, A. 1964. Review. Currall, H. F. *Gramophone record libraries: Their organization and practice. Bogens verden* 46: 181.
296. Burbridge, A. E. and Audsley, J. 1964. Review. Currall, H. F. *Gramophone record libraries: Their organization and practice. Library Association record* 66: 100-104.
297. Cunningham, Virginia A. 1964. The Library of Congress classed catalog for music. *Library resources & technical services* 8: 285-88.
298. Drake, Helen. 1964. Cataloging recordings. *Illinois libraries* 46: 145-52.
299. Hagen, Carlos B. 1964. *An information retrieval system for sound recordings.* Los Angeles: University of California.
300. Larrabee, B. B. 1964. Review. Currall, H. F. *Gramophone record libraries: Their organization and practice. Library quarterly* 34: 139-40.
301. Library of Congress. Descriptive Cataloging Division. 1964. *Rules for descriptive cataloging in the Library of Congress: Phonorecords.* Washington, D. C.: Library of Congress.
302. March, Ivan. 1964. Review. Currall, H. F. *Gramophone record libraries: Their organization and practice. North western newsletter* 79: 7-8.
303. Moon, Meredith M. 1964. Coloured cards for music in the Bodleian. *Brio* 1: 8, 17-18.
304. Moor, E. L. 1964. Review. Currall, H. F. *Gramophone record libraries: Their organization and practice. School librarian* 12: 43-44.
305. Oldman, C. B. 1964. Review. Currall, H. F. *Gramophone record libraries: Their organization and practice. Journal of documentation* 20: 101-2.
306. Ruden, Jan Olof. 1964. Kall-och litteraturforteckmung i musikvetenskapliga arbeten. *Svensk tidskrift for musikforskning* 46: 119-33.
307. Scholz, Dell DuBose. 1964. *Manual for the cataloging of recordings in public libraries.* Baton Rouge: Louisiana State University. Rev. ed.
308. Strange, A. 1964. Review. Currall, H. F. *Gramophone record libraries: Their organization and practice. Indexer* 4: 24.
309. United States Air Force Academy. 1964. *Phonograph record classification schedule.* Colorado Springs, Colo.: The Academy.
310. Vollans, R. F. 1964. Review. Currall, H. F. *Gramophone record libraries: Their organization and practice. Library review* 149: 350-351.

311. Whitehead, R. 1964. Review. Currall, H. F. *Gramophone record libraries: Their organization and practice. Australian library journal* 13: 34-35.
312. Zielinska, Bozena. 1964. O katalogowaniu nagran muzycyncych. *Przeglad biblioteczny* 32: 31-42.
313. Katalogisering af musikalier og grammofonplader; tillaef til katalogiseringsregler. 1965. Copenhagen: Bibliotekscentralen.
314. Klasifikacia hudby. 1965. *Slovenska hudba* 9: 394-95.
315. Review. Currall, H. F. *Gramophone record libraries: Their organization and practice*. 1965. *Journal of the International Folk Music Council* 17: 47.
316. Anderson, Sherman. 1965. Cataloging the contents of certain recordings. *Library resources & technical services* 9: 359-62.
317. Angell, Richard S. 1965. On the future of the Library of Congress classification. *Classification research: Proceedings of the Second International Study Conference*. Pauline Atherton, ed., 101-12. Copenhagen: Munksgaard.
318. Finney, T. M. 1965. Not in the B. U. C.: Lost in a binder's collection. *Notes* 21: 335-37.
319. Gohler, Albert. 1965. *Messkataloge im Dienste der musikalischen Geschichtsforschung: eine Anregung zur zeitgenössischen Bücherbeschreibung*. Hilversum: Frits A.M. Knuf. Reprint of dissertation. Leipzig, 1901. Catalogs of masses in the service of historical music research.
320. Hagen, Carlos B. 1965. A proposed information retrieval system for sound recordings. *Special libraries* 56: 223-28.
321. La Roche College Music Dept. 1965. *La Roche College classification system for phonorecords*. Allison Park, Pa.: La Roche College.
322. March, Ivan. 1965. *Running a record library*. Blackpool, Lancs. Long playing records library.
323. McColvin, Lionel R. and Reeves, Harold. 1965. *Music libraries*. London: Deutsch. Completely rewritten and extended by Jack Dove.
324. Musiol, Karol. 1965. *Opracowanie rzeczowe zbiorow muzycznych*. Katowice. Translation: Subject catalogs of the music library.
325. Ohm, B. 1965. Simplified cataloging: Here's one for the record. *Illinois libraries* 47: 120-32.
326. Pietro, Sister M. 1965. Recordings in the high school library. *Catholic library world* 37: 179-87.
327. Stevenson, Gordon. 1965. Music in medium-sized libraries. *Library journal* 90: 1255-58.

328. Stiles, Helen J. 1965. Phonograph record classification at the United States Air Force Academy Library. *Library resources & technical services* 9: 446-48.
329. Review. Currall, H. F. *Gramophone record libraries: Their organization and practice.* 1966. *Music review* 27: 151-52.
330. Review. Lapique, Becali Zoila. *Catalogación y classificación de la musica cubana.* 1966. *Ethomusicology* 10: 114+.
331. Review. Musiol, K. *Opracowanie rzeczowe zbiorow muzycznych.* 1966. *Muzyka* 11: 135-41.
332. Review. Redfern B. *Organizing music in libraries.* 1966. *Musical times* 107: 965-66.
333. Review. Redfern, B. *Organizing music in libraries.* 1966. *NATS* 23: 47.
334. Arntsen, Ella. 1966. Review. Redfern, Brian L. *Organizing music in libraries. Reol: nordisk bibliotekstidsskrift* 5, no. 3: 181-82.
335. Bradley, Carol June. 1966. *Manual of music librarianship.* Ann Arbor: Music Library Association.
336. Cazeaux, Isabelle. 1966. Classification and cataloging. In Carol June Bradley. *Manual of music librarianship*, 30-57. Ann Arbor, Mich.: Music Library Association.
337. Cunningham, Virginia A. 1966. Review. Redfern, B. *Organizing music in libraries. Notes* 23: 279-80.
338. Ellison, M. 1966. Review. Redfern, Brian L. Organizing music in libraries. *Pacific Northwest Library Association quarterly* 31: 116-17.
339. Geist, B. 1966. Hudebni prameny a jejich zpracovani. *Hudebni rozhledy* 19: 183.
340. Goldstein, Leba M. 1966. Pepys ballads. *Library (Bibilographical Society)* 21: 282-92.
341. Hammond, H. 1966. Punched card gramophone record catalogue at Luton Central Library. *Library world* 68: 168.
342. Hartman, E. R. 1966. Review. Redfern, Brian L. Organizing music in libraries. *Drexel library quarterly* 2: 398.
343. McGaw, Howard F. comp. 1966. Academic libraries using the LC classification system. *College & research libraries* 27: 31-36.
344. Morner, Carl Gabriel Stellen. 1966. De tryckta katalogkorten i teori och praktik. *Biblioteksbladet* 51: 755-56.
345. New York Public Library. Reference Department. 1966. *Music subject headings authorized for use in the catalogs of the Music Division.* Boston: G. K. Hall. 2nd ed., enl.

Chronological Listing

346. Redfern, Brian L. 1966. *Organizing music in libraries.* New York: Philosophical Library.
347. ———. 1966. *Organizing music in libraries.* London: Clive Bingley.
348. Steszewski, J. 1966. Prologomena do klasyfikacji ethnomuzykologicznych. *Muzyka* 11: 3-10.
349. Stevenson, W. B. 1966. Review. Redfern, Brian L. *Organizing music in libraries. Library world* 67: 356-57.
350. Thomas, Alan R. 1966. Review. Redfern, Brian L. *Organizing music in libraries. Library Association record* 68: 451.
351. Wassner, H. 1966. Katalogisieren von Musikalien an den öffentlichen Musikbüchereien. *Bücherei und Bild* 18: 625-27.
352. *Anglo-American cataloging rules.* 1967. Chicago: American Library Association.
353. Review. Gohler, A. *Die Messkataloge im Dienste der musikalischen Geschichtsforschung: Eine Anregung zur zeitgenossischen Bücherbeschreibung.* 1967. *Revue de musicologie* 53: 191-92. Catalogs of masses in the service of historical music research.
354. Review. Redfern, B. *Organizing music in libraries.* 1967. *Music educators journal* 54: 92-93.
355. Barnes, Christopher. 1967. Classification and cataloging of spoken records in academic libraries. *College & research libraries* 28: 49-52.
356. Cunningham, Virginia A. 1967. From Schmidt-Phiseldeck to Zanetti: Establishing an international cataloguing code for music. *Notes* 23: 449-52.
357. Daily, Jay E. 1967. The selection, processing, and storage of non-print materials: A critique of the Anglo-American cataloging rules as they relate to newer media. *Library trends* 16: 283-89.
358. Edmonton Public Library. 1967. *Classifying phonograph records using the Dewey decimal classifications: A section of the Edmonton Public Library cataloguing manual.* Edmonton: Edmonton Public Library.
359. Foss, G. 1967. A methodology for the description and classification of Anglo-American traditional tunes. *Journal of the Folklore Institute* 4: 102-26.

360. Hallgren, Sante. 1967. Finns det utrymme for specialservice? Problemet idealitet contra lonsamhet diskuteras med exempel fran produktionen av katalogkort till grammofonskivor. *Biblioteksbladet* 52: 603-5. Translation: Are special services possible? The ideal contra usefulness discussed with examples from the production of catalog cards for phonorecordings.
361. Jander, O. 1967. Staff-liner identification: A technique for the age of microfilm. *Journal of the American Musicological Society* 20: 112-16.
362. Millen, Irene. 1967. Review. Redfern, Brian L. *Organizing music in libraries. Library resources & technical services* 11: 122-24.
363. Morner, Carl Gabriel Stellen. 1967. Review.Redfern, Brian L. *Organizing music in libraries. Biblioteksbladet* 52, no. 1: 115.
364. Mrygon, Adam. 1967. Problemy katalogowania alfabetycznego drukow muzycznych. *Muzyka* 12: 46-60. Translation: Problems concerning the alphabetic cataloging of music prints.
365. Rochester, M. 1967. Review. Redfern, Brian L. *Organizing music in libraries. Australian library journal* 16: 34.
366. Schermall, H. 1967. Die deutsche Musik-Phonothek Phonoprisma. *Phonoprisma* 3: 68-71.
367. Regler for Klassificering og Opstilling af Grammofonplader. 1968. *Bogens verden* 50: 254-56.
368. Review. Redfern, B. *Organizing music in libraries*. 1968. *Brio* 3: 24-25.
369. Review. Redfern, B. *Organizing music in libraries*. 1968. *Instrumentalist* 22: 26.
370. Tableau de classification. 1968. *Bulletin d'informations de l'Association des bibliothécaires français* 13: 215-16.
371. Bradley, Carol June. 1968. *The Dickinson classification: A cataloging and classification manual for music: Including a reprint of the George Sherman Dickinson classification of musical compositions*. Carlisle, Pa.: Carlisle Books.
372. Bryant, Eric Thomas. 1968. Great Britain. *Fontes artis musicae* 15: 91-92.
373. Cunningham, Virginia A. 1968. Inside LC's Music Section. *Notes* 25: 205-8.
374. Cunningham, Virginia A. and Greener, B. R. 1968. United States of America. *Fontes artis musicae* 15: 97-99.
375. Dona, Mariangela. 1968. Italia. *Fontes artis musicae* 15: 92.
376. Forslin, A. 1968. Suomi. *Fontes artis musicae* 15: 97.
377. Gavalda, M. Q. 1968. España. *Fontes artis musicae* 15: 89.

Chronological Listing

378. Heckmann, Harald. 1968. *RISM*; Sitzung am 27. August 1967 in Salzburg. *Fontes artis musicae* 15: 45-47.
379. Kjellberg, E. 1968. En tematisk katalog med numericode-ett projekt vid SMA. *Svensk tidskrift for musikforskning* 50: 125-28. Translation: A thematic catalog with Numericode: A project at SMA (Swedish Archives of Music History).
380. Krohn, I. K. 1968. Ceskoslvensko. *Fontes artis musicae* 15: 84.
381. Musiol, Karol. 1968. Polska. *Fontes artis musicae* 15: 93-95.
382. Pethes, Ivan. 1968. The Classification of music and literature on music. *Fontes artis musicae* 15: 83-102.
383. ———. 1968. *A flexible classification system of music and literature on music*. Budapest: Centre of Library Science and Methodology.
384. Plesske, Hans-Martin. 1968. Deutsche Demokratische Republik. *Fontes artis musicae* 15: 87-88.
385. Rösner, Helmut. 1968. Deutschland: Bundesrepublik Deutschland. *Fontes artis musicae* 15: 85-87.
386. Tanno, J. 1968. Automation and music cataloging. *College music symposium* 8: 48-50.
387. Wallon, Simone. 1968. France. *Fontes artis musicae* 15: 89-91.
388. Winkel, E. 1968. Denmark. *Fontes artis musicae* 15: 84-5.
389. Wolff, H. C. 1968. Répertoire iconographique de l' opera (RICO). *Fontes artis musicae* 15: 50-51. Translation: Inventory of opera iconography (RICO).
390. Zehntner, H. 1968. Schweiz. *Fontes artis musicae* 15: 92-93.
391. Debat: g-Seddelfortegnelsen. 1969. *Bogens verden* 51: 142-43. Translation: Debate: phonograph card catalog.
392. Ahmad, Rashiduddin. 1969. Cataloguing of music. *Pakistan library review* 1/2(4) (1): 33-48.
393. Carey, John T. 1969. The visible index method of cataloging phonorecords. *Library resources & technical services* 13: 502-10.
394. Clavel, J. P. and Perret, L. D. 1969. Musique à la BCU de Lausanne. *Nachrichten (Vereinigung Schweizerische Bibliothekare)* 45: 57-64. Translation: Music at the BCU (Bibliothèque cantonale et universitaire).
395. Coover, James B. 1969. Computers, cataloguing, and co-operation. *Notes* 25: 437-46.
396. De Lerma, Dominique-René. 1969. Philosophy and practice of phonorecord classification at Indiana University. *Library resources & technical services* 13: 86-92.
397. Goodfriend, J. 1969. On filing records. *Stereo review* 22: 44+.

398. Hamilton, D. 1969. Now where did I put that Franck Sonata? *High fidelity* 19: 56-60.
399. List, George Harold 1969. A statement on archiving. *Journal of the Folklore Institute* 6: 222-31.
400. Phillips, Don. 1969. An expandable classification scheme for phonorecord libraries. *Library resources & technical services* 13: 511-15.
401. Saheb-Ettaba, C. and McFarland, R. B. 1969. *ANSCR: The alphanumeric system for classification of recordings*. Williamsport, Pa.: Bro-Dart.
402. Schiodt, Nanna. 1969. EDB-registrering af grammofonplader. *Bogens verden* 51: 317-18.
403. Smith, L. 1969. Om klassificering og opstilling af grammofonplader. *Bogens verden* 51: 26.
404. Sunder, Mary Jane. 1969. Organization of recorded sound. *Library resources & technical services* 13: 93-98.
405. Tischler, Hans. 1969. And what is musicology? *Musical times* 30: 253-60. Includes table designating subjects and methods of whole field and appendix listing previous system of musicology.
406. Volkersz, Evert J. 1969. Neither book nor manuscript: Some special collections. *Library resources & technical Services* 13: 493-501.
407. Whiting, Bernard C. 1969. *A classification for Baroque music*. Liverpool: Liverpool School of Librarianship.
408. Kostnader for katalogisering av grammofonskivor. 1970. *Biblioteksbladet* 55: 57-59. Translation: Cost of cataloging recordings.
409. Review. Langridge, D. W. *Your jazz collection*. 1970. *Jazz journal* 23: 15+.
410. Review. Langridge, D. W. *Your jazz collection*. 1970. *Matrix* 89: 15.
411. Review. Langridge, D. W. *Your jazz collection*. 1970. *Melody maker* 45: 31.
412. Review. Whiting, B. C. *A classification for Baroque music*. 1970. *Notes* 27: 28.
413. Bjornum, Ove. 1970. I anledning af Freddy Larsens kritiske bemærkininger om Gruppe 78 i DK 5. udgave. *Bogens verden* 52: 523-25. Translation: On the occasion of Freddy Larsen's critical remarks on group 78 in DK 5th ed.: Reply.

414. Currall, Henry F. J. 1970. *Gramophone record libraries: Their organization and practice.* London: C. Lockwood. 2nd ed. At head of title: The International Association of Music Libraries, United Kingdom Branch.
415. Currall, Henry F. J. 1970. *Phonograph record libraries.* Hamden, Conn.: Archon. At head of title: The International Association of Music Libraries, United Kingdom Branch.
416. Eskew, Harry. 1970. Using early American hymnals and tunebooks. *Notes* 27: 19-23.
417. Grafton, Derek. 1970. BBC Gramophone Library cataloguing practice. *Phonograph Record Libraries: Their Organisation and Practice.* 2nd ed., Henry F. J. Currall, 57-64. London: Crosby Lockwood.
418. Halberg, Per. 1970. *Musik pa bibliotek: En handbok for det dagliga arbetet.* Lund: Bibliotekstjanst. Translation: Music in the library: A handbook for daily tasks.
419. Hilton, Ruth. 1970. Review. Saheb-Ettaba, C. and McFarland, R. B. *ANSCR: The alpha-numeric system for classification of recordings. Notes* 27: 52-54.
420. Hitchon, Jean C. 1970. Indicators. *Phonograph record libraries: Their organisation and practice.* 2nd ed., Henry F. J. Currall, 80-83. London: Crosby Lockwood and Son, Ltd.
421. Krohn, Ernst C. 1970. On classifying sheet music. *Notes* 26: 473-78.
422. Langridge, Derek Wilton. 1970. *Your jazz collection.* Hamden, Conn: Archon Books.
423. Larsen, Freddy. 1970. Musikdebat: Gruppe 78 i DK 5. udgave: nogle kritiske bemaevkninger. *Bogens verden* 52: 521-23. Translation: Music debate: Group 78 in DK 5th ed.: Some critical remarks.
424. Library of Congress. 1970. *Rules for the brief cataloging of music in the Library of Congress: Exceptions to the Anglo-American cataloging rules.* Washington, D.C.: Library of Congress.
425. Mason, Eric. 1970. Keeping track. *Music and musicians* 18: 50.
426. Miller, Miriam. 1970. AACR, 1967: Chapters 13 & 14: A music librarian's view of a cataloguing code. *Brio* 7: 27-31.
427. Wienpahl, Robert W. 1970. Re-cataloging a college score and phonorecords collection. *Library resources & technical services* 14: 421-27.
428. Woods, R. 1970. Report on national program archives. *ARSC journal* 2: 3-23.
429. Smolian, Steve. 1970-1971. A new development in printed catalog cards for records. *ARSC journal* 3: 33-37.

430. 1970-. *Music cataloging bulletin*. Ann Arbor, Mich.: Music Library Association. Vol. 1, no. 1 (Jan. 1970).
431. Indexing system can catalogue 10,000 records. 1971. *High fidelity* 21: 34-35.
432. Music classification numbers (extract from *Cataloging service bulletin 90*). 1971. *Library of Congress information bulletin* 30 (Jan. 14): 1.
433. Arntsen, Ella. 1971. Review. Currall, H. F. *Gramophone record libraries: Their organization and practice.* 2nd ed. *Scandinavian public library quarterly* 4, no. 2: 123-24.
434. British Standards Institution. 1971. *Specification for the presentation of bibliographical information in printed music.* London: The Institution.
435. Cunningham, Virginia A. 1971. *Rules for full cataloging.* Frankfurt; New York: C. F. Peters. Regles de catalogage détaillé, traduction de Yvette Fédoroff = Regeln für die vollständige Titelaufnahme, Übersetzung von Kurt Dortmüller; *Code international de Catalogage de la musique* v. 3
436. Flint, J. M. 1971. Review. Currall, H. F. *Gramophone record libraries: Their organization and practice.* 2nd ed. *Australian library journal* 20: 43.
437. Lenneberg, Hans. 1971. Dating engraved music: the present state of the art. *Library quarterly* 41: 128-40.
438. Lindberg, F. 1971. Datorbaserad katalogisering av grammofonskivor. *Bogens verden* 53: 386-95.
439. Lindner, Richard John. 1971. "Critiques: A cataloging technique and a computer aided system for retrieving information about brass music." University of Iowa. Ph.D. thesis.
440. Patterson, Charles Darold. 1971. "Graphemic, morphological, syntactical, lexical and context analysis of the Library of Congress music subject headings and their relationship to the Library of Congress classification schedule, class M, as determined by a comparative sampling of their two vocabularies." University of Pittsburgh. Ph.D. thesis.
441. Taylor, R. T. 1971. Cataloging the music library. *Instrumentalist* 25: 20.
442. Volek, Jaroslav. 1971. Vers un taxonomie de l'art. *Revue d'esthetique* 24: 2-16.
443. Class numbers for records. 1972. *Library of Congress information bulletin* 31: 70.
444. Commission de travail. 1972. *Fontes artis musicae* 19: 163-91.

Chronological Listing 59

445. Allen, Daniel. 1972. 78 rpm phonorecords in the Jazz Archive. *Institute of Professional Librarians of Ontario quarterly* 13: 119-61.
446. Bradley, Carol June. 1972. The Dickinson classification for music: An introduction. *Fontes artis musicae* 19: 13-22.
447. Derbyshire, Joseph J. 1972. LC music headings [letter]. *Library Journal* 97: 3257-58.
448. Foster, Donald L. 1972. *The classification of nonbook materials in academic libraries: A commentary and bibliography.* Urbana-Champaign: University of Illinois Library. Occasional paper no. 104.
449. Hall, D. 1972. Record industry notes. *Notes* 28: 667-68.
450. Hubbard, Lee. 1972. Records ain't what they used to be: Record classification. *Unabashed librarian* 4: 30-31.
451. Maruyama, L. S. and Avram, H. D. 1972. Cataloging and the computer. *Fontes artis musicae* 19: 164-71.
452. McFarland, Roger B. 1972. Phonorecord classification. *Bibliographic control of nonprint media.*, 374-77. Chicago: American Library Association.
453. Miller, Philip L. 1972. Review. Currall, H. F. *Gramophone record libraries: Their organization and practice.* 2nd ed. *Notes* 28: 449-50.
454. ———. 1972. Review. Currall, H. F. *Gramophone record libraries: Their organization and practice.* 2nd ed. *Notes* 28: 449.
455. Neumann, Klaus L. 1972. Efforts in West German radio to harmonize cataloguing instructions. *Fontes artis musicae* 19: 179-80.
456. Robbins, Donald C. 1972. Current resources for the bibliographic control of sound recordings. *Library trends* 21: 136-46.
457. Schiodt, Nanna. 1972. Checklist for cataloguing music manuscripts and prints. *Fontes artis musicae* 19: 171-74.
458. Scilken, Marvin H. 1972. Public library phonorecord system. *Unabashed librarian* 2: 10-11.
459. Stevenson, Gordon. 1972. Trends in archival and reference collections of recorded sound. *Library trends* 21, no. 1. Special issue edited by Gordon Stevenson.
460. Varga, Ovidiu. 1972. Specificonostmuzike i njeno u klasifikaciji umetnosti. *Zvuk* 121-23: 151-54. Translation: Specific features of music and its place in the classification of the arts.
461. Volek, Jaroslav. 1972. Hudba jako predmet sdeleni. *Hudebni veda* 9: 225-36; 304-317. Suggests a new classification system for the international decimal classification of music and music literature.
462. Bradley, Carol June. 1973. *Reader in music librarianship.* Washington, D.C.: NCR Microcard Books.

463. Brown, Andrew F. David. 1973. Organizing your music library. *School musician* 44: 40-41.
464. Bryant, Eric Thomas. 1973. Sound recordings & N. B. M. rules. *Catalogue & index* 31: 6-7.
465. Claesson, Inge. 1973. Nya katalogiseringsmetoder vid Sveriges Radios (SR:s) Grammofonarkiv. *Biblioteksbladet* 58: 250.
466. Deutscher Bibliotheksverband. Arbeitskreis öffentliche Musikbibliotheken. Kommision für Tonträger-Systematik. 1973. *Tonträger-Systematik Musik für öffentliche Musikbibliotheken.* Berlin: Deutscher Bibliotheksverband, Arbeitsstelle für das Bibliothekswesen.
467. Music. 1973. *Special cataloguing: With particular reference to music, films, maps, serials, and the multi-media computerised catalogue.* John Leonard Horner, 30-130. London: Clive Bingley.
468. Music. 1973. *Special cataloguing: With particular reference to music, films, maps, serials, and the multi-media computerised catalogue.* John Leonard Horner, 30-130. Hamden, Conn.: Linnet Books.
469. Massil, S. W. 1973. Music in an automated cataloguing system using MARC. *Brio* 10: 1-4.
470. Music Library Association. Cataloging and classification committee. 1973. *SLACC: The partial use of the shelf list as a classed catalog.* Ann Arbor, Mich.: Music Library Association. MLA technical reports, no. 1.
471. Novikova, Elena Andreevna. 1973. Kak opisyvat' noty i zvukozapisi. *Bibliotekar'* 5: 62. Translation: Cataloging of music and recordings.
472. Rosenberg, Kenyon Charles. 1973. State of record cataloging. *Library journal/School library journal previews*: 5-11.
473. Skrobela, Katherine C. 1973. On LC music headings. *Library journal* 98: 484. Letter in reply to J. J. Derbyshire.
474. Computerized cataloging project for archival sound recordings. 1974. *Notes* 31: 281.
475. Blacker, George A. 1974. A proposed standard discographical data sheet. *Record Research* 125-126: 12-13.
476. Buth, Olga. 1974. Scores and recordings. *Library trends* 23: 427-50.
477. Cipolla, Wilma Reid. 1974. Music subject headings: A comparison. *Library resources & technical services* 18: 387-97.
478. Foreman, Lewis. 1974. *Systematic discography.* London: Shoe String.

479. Henderson, Ruth. 1974. Subject heads: A rebuttal (letter). *Library journal* 99: 3156-57.
480. Koltypina, Galina B. and Nevraev, V. IU. 1974. Nekotorye osobennosti modele bibliograficheskoi zapisi i sistemy kodirovanila notnykh izdanii. *Sovetskoe bibliotekovedenie* 2: 47-57.
481. Krummel, Donald W. 1974. *Guide for dating early published music: A manual of bibliographical practices.* Hackensack, N.J.: J. Boonin.
482. Lindberg, F. 1974. Gramophone record catalogues based on EDP routines: A short survey. *Fontes artis musicae* 21: 28-32.
483. Miles, Robert. 1974. Cataloging and classification of music on phonorecords: Some considerations. *Library resources & technical services* 18: 213-19.
484. Rasmussen, Mary. 1974. Establishing an index of musical instruments and musical subjects in works of Western art: Some personal suggestions. *Notes* 30: 460-73.
485. ———. 1974. Establishing an index of musical instruments and musical subjects in works of Western art: Some personal suggestions. *Library science with a slant to documentation* 30: 78.
486. Rklitskala, A. and Khasanova, N. 1974. Katalogl fonoteki konsul'tatsiia. *Bibliotekar* 3: 55-56.
487. Spear, Horace L. 1974. A proposed standard discographical data sheet. *Record research* 127: 5.
488. Spence, T. 1974. Toward the ideal archival catalog. *Journal of jazz studies* 1: 97-106.
489. Library of Congress. 1974-. *Name headings with references.* Washington, D.C.: The Library.
490. *Proceedings of the Institute on Library of Congress Music Cataloging Policies and Procedures.* 1975. Ann Arbor, Mich.: Music Library Association. MLA technical reports, no. 3.
491. Baader, Peter. 1975. Uniform titles for liturgical works. *International cataloguing* 4: 6-7.
492. Campbell, A. B. 1975. Organizing the Brevard College Music Library. *North Carolina libraries* 33: 22-26.
493. Clews, J. P. 1975. Revision of DC 780; the Phoenix schedule. *Brio* 12: 7-14.
494. Daily, Jay E. 1975. Cataloging of phonorecords. *Library resources & technical services* 19: 421. Letter in reply to R. Miles.
495. ———. 1975. *Cataloging phonorecordings: Problems and possibilities.* New York: Marcel Dekker.

496. ———. 1975. Comment: Miles, R. Cataloging and classification of music on phonorecords: Some considerations. *Library resources & technical services* 19: 421.
497. International Federation of Library Associations. Working Group on Uniform Headings for Liturgical Works. 1975. *List of uniform titles for liturgical works of the Latin rites of the Catholic Church.* London: International Federation of Library Associations.
498. Limbacher, J. L. 1975. Review. Daily, Jay E. *Cataloging phonorecordings: problems and possibilities. Library journal* 100: 1484.
499. Martinez-Göllner, Marie Louise. 1975. *Rules for cataloging music manuscripts.* Frankfurt; New York: C.F. Peters. Regles de catalogage des manuscrits musicaux = Regeln für die Katalogisierung von Musikhandschriften; Code international de catalogage de la musique v. 4.
500. Musiol, Karol. 1975. Sonderkataloge für Musiksammlungen; aus der Praxis einer öffentlichen Hochschulbibliothek. *Musikbibliothek Aktuell* 3-4: 134-45.
501. Newbould, Brian. 1975. A question of identity. *Musical opinion and music trade review* 99: 69.
502. Pfeiffer, G. 1975. Information zur Systematik für Musikschallplatten. *Bibliothekar* 29: 245-46.
503. Stevenson, Gordon. 1975. Collectors, catalogs and libraries. *ARSC Journal* 7: 21-32.
504. ———. 1975. Review. Daily, Jay E. *Cataloging phonorecordings: problems and possibilities. College & research libraries* 36: 429-30.
505. Stoakley, Roger J. 1975. West Sussex catalogue of recorded sounds. *Program* 9: 95.
506. Youngblood, J. 1975. Review. Lindner, Richard John *Critiques: A cataloging technique and a computer aided system for retrieving information about brass music. Council for Research in Music Education bulletin* 44: 18-22.
507. *Anglo-American cataloging rules. Chapter 14 revised: Sound recordings.* 1976. Chicago: American Library Association.
508. Research on nonbook materials undertaken by the British Library. 1976. *Information hotline* 8: 5.
509. Andrewes, Richard. 1976. Review. Martinez-Göllner, Marie Louise. *Rules for cataloging music manuscripts. Brio* 13: 56-58.
510. Bellord, Julia. 1976. Uniform titles for liturgical works. *Bulletin of the Association of British Theological and Philosophical Libraries* 6: 13-16.

Chronological Listing

511. Benton, Rita. 1976. The nature of music and some implications for the university music library. *Fontes artis musicae* 23: 53-60.
512. Culshaw, J. 1976. The advantages of disorder. *High fidelity* 26: 16+.
513. Dowell, Arlene Taylor. 1976. *Cataloging with copy: A decision-maker's handbook.* Littleton, Colo.: Libraries Unlimited.
514. Ducasse, Henri and Pages, Denys. 1976. Systeme de constitution et d'exploitation données pour l'identification et l'analyse de textes musicaux. *Revue de musicologie* 62: 292-93. Translation: A system of formatting and processing data for the identification and analysis of musical texts.
515. Enkstrom, Ann. 1976. Nonprint materials in the OCLC data base. *Ohio Association of School Librarians bulletin* 5: 24.
516. Graydon, Alec. 1976. The numbers racket. *Crescendo international* 15: 13.
517. Jones, Malcolm. 1976. Printed music and the MARC format. *Program* 10: 119-22.
518. Keyser, P. 1976. Records: How to arrange your collection. *Clavier* 15: 30-33.
519. Kirchberg, Klaus. 1976. Review. Martinez-Göllner, Marie Louise. *Rules for cataloging music manuscripts. Musica* 30: 338-39.
520. Krummel, Donald W. 1976. Musical functions and bibliographical forms. *Library (Bibilographical Society)* 5th ser. v. 31: 327-50.
521. Lewis, D. 1976. Record libraries commission. *Fontes artis musicae* 23: 77-80.
522. Library of Congress. MARC Development Office. 1976. *Music: A MARC format.* Washington, D. C.: Library of Congress.
523. Mills, Patrick. 1976. What ISBD is all about. *Brio* 13: 30-31.
524. Mullally, George P. 1976. Some remarks on the Library of Congress classification schedule for music. *Fontes artis musicae* 23: 60-61.
525. Schiodt, Nanna. 1976. MUSICAT: A method of cataloguing music manuscripts by computer, as applied in the Danish RISM manuscript project. *Fontes artis musicae* 23: 158-66.
526. ———. 1976. Musik, EDB og gtode Programmorer. *Bibliotek* 70: 212-23.
527. Sweeney, Russell. 1976. Music in the Dewey decimal classification. *Catalogue & Index* 42: 4-6.
528. British Library: Pilot experiment on a national cataloguing service for non-book materials. 1976-1977. *Audiovisual librarian* 3: 78.
529. Automated music. 1977. *Library Association record* 79: 457.

530. Neues System für Registratur und Archiv. 1977. *Musikhandel* 28: 240.
531. Review. Gaeddert, B. *The classification and cataloguing of sound recordings: An annotated bibliography.* 1977. *Notes* 34: 88.
532. Andrew, Janet Ruth. 1977. *Developments in the organisation of non-book materials.* London: Aslib. Papers and proceedings of a seminar on developments in the organisation and availability of non-book materials held at the Library Association on 18th November 1976.
533. Bowles, Garrett H. 1977. The AAA project. *ARSC journal* 9: 16-25.
534. Gaeddert, B. 1977. *The classification and cataloguing of sound recordings: An annotated bibliography.* Ann Arbor, Mich.: Music Library Association.
535. Kaufman, Judith. 1977. *Recordings of non-Western music: Subject and added entry access.* Ann Arbor, Mich.: Music Library Association. MLA technical reports no. 5.
536. Kirstein, Finn and Smith-Nielsen, Claus. 1977. MUSICAT: A technical description of the Danish music cataloguing project. *Fontes artis musicae* 24: 69-71.
537. Kokkonen, Oili 1977. Musikkiiluettelointi harhailee. *Kirjastolehti* 70: 214-6.
538. Miller, Miriam. 1977. Computer cataloguing and the broadcasting library. *Fontes artis musicae* 24: 74-75.
539. Rangra, V. K. 1977. Name pattern of indian musicians and choice of entry element. *Library science with a slant to documentation* 14: 124-28.
540. Wennering, H. 1977. Att katalogisera skivor. *Musikrevy* 32: 287.
541. Werkhoven, H. B. van. 1977. The automation plans of the music library of the Nederlandse Omroep Stichting—Dutch Broadcasting Foundation. *Fontes artis musicae* 24: 72-74.
542. Review. Andrew, J. ed. *Developments in the organisation of non-book materials.* 1978. *Recorded sound* 70-71: 810-11.
543. Review. Gaeddert, B. *The classification and cataloguing of sound recordings: An annotated bibliography.* 1978. *Musical times* 119: 424.
544. Review. Redfern, B. L. *Organizing music in libraries vol. 1: Arrangement and classification.* 1978. *Music in education* 45: 488.
545. Bindman, Fred. 1978. ISBD (Music) progress reported. *Library of Congress information bulletin* 37: 339.
546. Canby, Edward Tatnall. 1978. Audio. *Audio* 62: 22+.

Chronological Listing

547. Chan, T. S. 1978. Organizing jazz records: A listener's viewpoint. *Singapore libraries* 8: 24-25.
548. Elfers, J. 1978. "Manual of examples of music cataloging." Kent State University. Research paper.
549. Hammond, Merrill M. 1978. Jazz record collecting—A hot romance. *Second line* 30, Spring: 12-18; Summer: 12-18; Fall: 5-13; Winter: 41-44.
550. Hoffmann, H. K. 1978. Choice of main entry for sound recordings. *International cataloguing* 7: 5-7.
551. Johansson, Corry. 1978. New numericode thematic catalogue in the library of the Royal Swedish Academy of Music in Stockholm. *Fontes artis musicae* 25: 52-55.
552. Jones, Peter Ward. 1978. Review. Martinez-Göllner, Marie Louise. *Rules for cataloging music manuscripts. Music & letters* 3: 359.
553. Lanzke, Heinz. 1978. ISBD (Music): First meeting of the IFLA/IAML Working Group in Mainz, 29-21 September 1977. *Fontes artis musicae* 25: 105.
554. Library of Congress. 1978. *Classification class M: Music and books on music*. Washington, D.C.: The Library.
555. Pinion, Catherine F. 1978. The impact of non-book materials—with particular reference to music libraries. *Fontes artis musicae* 25: 227-30.
556. Redfern, Brian L. 1978. *Organizing music in libraries vol. 1: Arrangement and classification*. London; Hamden, Conn.: Bingley; Linnet.
557. Smith, Ruth S. 1978. Cataloging sound recordings. *Cataloging made easy: How to organize your congregation's library.* New York: Seabury Press.
558. Steuermann, Clara. 1978. Music libraries. *Special libraries* 69: 425-28.
559. Sundin, Tommy. 1978. Ge oss Regler für Notkatalogisering (letter). *Biblioteksbladet* 63: 20. Translation: Give us rules for music cataloging.
560. Unger, I. 1978. Zur Einführung der Klassification für Tonträger/Musik. *Bibliothekar* 32: 112-16.
561. Redfern, Brian L. 1978. *Organising music in libraries*. London; Hamden, Conn.: Bingley; Linnet.
562. Bibliographic control of printed music. 1979. *International cataloguing* 8: 18-24.
563. Review. Jones, M. *Music librarianship*. 1979. *Brio* 16: 42.

564. Allison, A. M. and Lawrence, J. E. 1979. *Chorlist*—computerized index to choral octavo scores. *Collection management*: 79-96.
565. Birmingham Libraries Cooperative Mechanisation Project (BLCMP). 1979. Study into the effects of AACR2 on music MARC catalogues: Preliminary report from the BLCMP Music Group. *Brio* 16: 38-41.
566. Bruhns, S. et al. 1979. *Haandbog i musikbiblioteksarbejde*. Bibliotekscentralens forlag.
567. Canby, Edward Tatnall. 1979. Audio, etc. *Audio* 63: 26+. "How music of the time influenced building of concert halls"—c.f. Music index online.
568. Coral, Lenore. 1979. Review. Library of Congress. *Classification class M: Music and books on music* 3rd ed. *Notes* 35: 892-92.
569. Geering, M. 1979. Weitere Entwicklung der Arbeit an ISBD (PM), ehemals ISBD (Music). *Nachrichten (Vereinigung Schweizerische Bibliothekare)* 55: 60-61. Translation: Further development of the work on ISBD(PM), formerly ISBD (Music).
570. Gray, Michael. 1979. Discography: Its prospects and problems. *Notes* 35: 578-92.
571. Heckmann, Harald. 1979. Computer aids in music libraries and archives. *Fontes artis musicae* 26: 100-101.
572. Hoffmann, Frank W. 1979. Arrangement and classification of sound recordings. *Development of library collections of sound recordings*. Frank W. Hoffmann, 91-104. New York: M. Dekker.
573. Jones, Malcolm. 1979. *Music librarianship*. London: Bingley. Chapter 6: Library organization and routines: processing.
574. King, Alexander Hyatt. 1979. *Printed music in the British Museum: An account of the collections, the catalogues, and their formation up to 1920*. London; New York: Clive Bingley; K. G. Saur.
575. Kleteckova, Marie. 1979. K nekterym otazkam soupisu a popisu starych notovanych kniznichy pamatek. *Knihovna vedeckoteoreticky sbornik* 21: 343-48.
576. Mills, P. 1979. Supplement for ISBD enthusiasts. *Brio* 16: 37-38.
577. Prokopowicz, Maria. 1979. Traditions and achievements of music libraries and library science in the Polish People's Republic. *Fontes artis musicae* 26: 36-43.
578. Ravilious, C. P. 1979. AACR2 and its implications for music cataloguing. *Brio* 16: 2-12.
579. Redfern, Brian L. 1979. *Organizing music in libraries vol. 2: Cataloging*. London; Hamden, Conn.: Bingley; Linnet.

Chronological Listing

580. Rösing, Helmut. 1979. RISM-Handschriftenkatalogisierung und elektronische Datenverarbeitung (EDV). *Fontes artis musicae* 26: 107-9. Translation: RISM manuscript cataloging and electronic data processing (EDV).
581. Spalding, C. Sumner. 1979. Music authority files at the Library of Congress. *Music cataloging bulletin* 10: 4-6.
582. Unger, I. 1979. Klassifikation Tonträger/Musik—auch für Kinderbibliotheken. *Bibliothekar* 33: 456-57. Translation: The category "recorded music" is also for children's libraries.
583. Wassner, Hermann. 1979. *Musikleben und Musikbibliothek; Beiträge zur musikbibliothekarischen Arbeit der Gegenwart, vorgelegt anlässlich des 75-järigen Bestehens der öffentlichen Musikbibliothek in Frankfurt am Main*. Berlin: Deutscher Bibliotheksverband. Translation: Musical life and the music library: Essays on present-day music librarianship.
584. *DDC, Dewey decimal classification proposed revision of 780 music: Based on Dewey decimal classification and relative index*. 1980. Albany, N.Y.: Forest Press. Prepared under the direction of Russell Sweeney and John Clews with assistance from Winton E. Matthews.
585. Review. Bruhns, S. et al. 1980. Handbog i musikbiblioteksarbejde. *Dansk musiktidsskrift* 55: 92-93.
586. Review. King, A. H. 1980. *Printed music in the British Museum: An account of the collections, the catalogues, and their formation up to 1920*. *Musical times* 121: 319.
587. Review. Redfern, B. L. 1980. *Organizing music in libraries vol. 2: Cataloging*. *Brio* 17: 22-25.
588. Review. Redfern, B. L. 1980. *Organizing music in libraries vol. 2: Cataloging*. *Music teacher* 59: 29.
589. Review. Redfern, B. L. 1980. *Organizing music in libraries*. Rev. ed. *Music teacher* 59: 29.
590. Working group offers review of ISBD for non-book materials. 1980. *Library of Congress information bulletin* 39: 439-40.
591. Campbell, Freda. 1980. APPARAT: A computer cataloguing system for sound recordings. *Archives and manuscripts* 8: 33-40.
592. Coral, Lenore. 1980. Open session on ISBD (NBM), Salzburg 4 July 1979. *Fontes artis musicae* 27: 20.
593. Dona, Mariangela. 1980. Regole di catalogazione della musica e dei documenti sonori. *Bollettino d'informazioni (Associazione Italiana Biblioteche)* 20: 265-70.
594. Dorfmüller, Kurt. 1980. Klassifikationsprobleme bei Musikalien Sachstandsbericht. *Forum Musikbibliothek* 4: 18-22.

595. Funabiki, Ruth P. and Van Ausdal, Karl. 1980. *The music OCLC users group tagging workbook and reference manual.* Newton, Mass.: Nelinet.
596. Griffin, Marie. 1980. IJS jazz register and indexes: a COM catalog of the recorded sound collection of the Rutgers Institute of Jazz Studies. *Library of Congress information bulletin* 39: 126-28.
597. Hassell, Robert Hanks. 1980. "Music in the library: A comparative analysis of several classification schemes." University of Chicago. M.A. thesis.
598. Hinton, Frances. 1980. Cartographic materials, manuscripts, music, and sound recordings. *Making of a code: The issues underlying AACR 2.* Chicago: American Library Association. Papers given at the International Conference on AACR 2, held March 11-14, 1979 in Tallahassee, Florida.
599. Lanzke, Heinz. 1980. Zur Entstehung der Musikalien-sonderregeln zu RAK. *Forum Musikbibliothek* 1: 46-52.
600. Redfern, Brian L. 1980. *Organizing music in libraries.* Hamden, Conn.: Shoestring.
601. Research Libraries Group, Inc. 1980. *MARC tagging workbook: Scores.* Stanford, Calif.: Research Libraries Group.
602. ———. 1980. *MARC tagging workbook: Sound recordings.* Stanford, Calif.: Research Libraries Group.
603. Stoessel, K. 1980. Computereinsatz in der Musikkatalogisierung im Deutschen Rundfunkarchiv. *Fontes artis musicae* 27: 178-83. Translation: Computer applications in music cataloging in the Deutsches Rundfunkarchiv.
604. Swan, J. 1980. Sound archives: The role of the collector and the library. *ARSC Journal* 12: 8-17.
605. ISBD (NBM)—Sound recording; amendments and additions. 1981. *Fontes artis musicae* 28: 63-67.
606. Music of ethnic and national groups. 1981. *Music cataloging bulletin* 12, no. 5: 2-4.
607. Review. Redfern, B. L. 1981. *Organizing music in libraries. Music educators journal* 67: 29.
608. Review. Wassner, H. ed. 1981. *Musikleben und Musikbibliothek. Musik und Kirche* 51: 93-94. Translation: Musical life and the music library: Essays on present-day music librarianship.
609. Review. Wassner, H. ed. 1981. *Musikleben und Musikbibliothek. Musikforschung* 34: 341. Translation: Musical life and the music library: Essays on present-day music librarianship.

Chronological Listing

610. Review. Wassner, H., ed. 1981. *Musikleben und Musikbibliothek. Musica* 35: 56-57. Translation: Musical life and the music library: Essays on present-day music librarianship.
611. Sound archives indexing (of 78s on file). 1981. *Billboard* 93: 60.
612. Baer, Eckehard. 1981. Zum Aufbau des Einheitssachtitels für Musikalien und Tonträger—am Beispiel des Deutschen Musikarchivs Berlin. *Fontes artis musicae* 28: 56-58. Translation: Toward the development of a uniform title for printed and recorded music: Using the example of the Deutsche Musikarchiv, Berlin.
613. Bean, Charles W. 1981. "An index of folksongs contained in theses and dissertations in the Library of Congress, Washington D.C." Loughborough University of Technology, Department of Library and Information Studies. Dissertation.
614. Berman, Sanford. 1981. Let there be music (but not too soon). *Joy of cataloging:* 86-89. Oryx Press.
615. Bowles, Garrett H. 1981. Automated bibliographic control of music. *The information community: An alliance for progress.* Lunin, Lois F. et al., eds. White Plains, N.Y.: AIS.
616. Bradley, Carol June. 1981. *Music collection in American libraries: A chronology.* Detroit: Information Coordinators.
617. Bradley, Carol June. 1981. The Music Library Association: The founding generation and its work. *Notes* 37: 763-822.
618. Dillon, Martin et al. 1981. Use of automatic indexing for authority control. *Journal of library automation* 14: 268-77.
619. Dorfmüller, Kurt. 1981. Form- und Gattungsnamen im Sach-katalog der musica practica; zum Entwarf eines Thesaurus. *Fontes artis musicae* 28: 115-29. Translation: Form and generic names in subject catalogs for music: Model for a thesaurus.
620. Eick, B. et al. 1981. A discotopology primer. *ARSC journal* 13: 4-19.
621. Godfrey, Marlene. 1981. Jazz and reggae at Trinity and All Saints College. *Audiovisual librarian* 7: 14.
622. Gorman, Hester. 1981. Contemporary music at Trinity and All Saints College. *Audiovisual librarian* 7: 15-16.
623. International Federation of Library Associations. Working Group on Uniform Headings for Liturgical Works. 1981. *List of uniform titles for liturgical works of the Latin rites of the Catholic Church.* London: International Federation of Library Associations. 2nd ed., rev.
624. Jones, A. 1981. Survival through coordination: The future development of libraries. *Brio* 18: 1-3.

625. Kan, I. 1981. Bibliograficheskoe Opisanie Notnykg Izdanii. *Bibliotekar* 4: 60-61.
626. Kobayashi, Mari. 1981. Notes on improvement of the indexing of musical themes. *Library and information science* 19: 136-50.
627. Kotherova, E. 1981. Czech music libraries. *Music news from Prague* 4: 1-2.
628. Liebman, Roy. 1981. The media index: Computer-based access to nonprint materials. *Reference quarterly* 20: 291-99.
629. Luke, Karl. 1981. Katalogisierung von Musik-Tonträgern in einer Rundfunkanstalt. *Forum Musikbibliothek* 2: 69-78.
630. Olson, Nancy B. 1981. *Cataloging of audiovisual materials: A manual based on AACR2*. Mankato, Minn.: Minnesota Scholarly Press.
631. Opsal, Tua Standahl. 1981. Musikkbibliotekarene venter pa ny oversettelse av katalogiseringsreglene. *Bok og bibliotek* 48: 505. Translation: The music librarians are waiting for a new translation of the cataloguing rules.
632. Reimer, Jürgen. 1981. Fragen der statistischen Erfassung von Musikalien. *Forum Musikbibliothek* 2: 92-99.
633. Sass, Herbert. 1981. Zur Dokumentation des Musiklebens der Gegenwart, national und international. *Forum Musikbibliothek* 4: 218-44. Translation: Concerning the documentation of present day musical activity on a national and international level.
634. Sawkins, Lionel. 1981. Encore to the *Lexicographer's dilemma*, or de Lalande et du Bon Sens. *Fontes artis musicae* 28: 319-23.
635. Smiraglia, Richard P. 1981. *AACR2*: The first year at Urbana. *Notes* 37: 712-15.
636. ———. 1981. *Shelflisting music: Guidelines for use with Library of Congress classification: M*. Philadelphia: Music Library Association. MLA technical reports, no. 9.
637. Smiraglia, Richard P. and Papakhian, Arsen Ralph. 1981. Music in the OCLC online union catalog: A review. *Notes* 38: 257-74.
638. Smiraglia, Richard P. and Papakhian, Arsen Ralph. 1981. Music in the OCLC online union catalog: A review erratum. *Notes* 38: 968.
639. Snekkenes, Gudrun. 1981. Platebiblioteket i NRK—over 100,000 plater. *Bok og bibliotek* 48: 502-4.
640. Stevenson, Gordon. 1981. Music librarianship in the United States. *Advances in librarianship v. 11.*, 163-206. New York: Academic Press.
641. Watanabe, Ruth. 1981. American music libraries and librarianship: An overview in the eighties. *Notes* 38: 239-56.

642. Anlass, Zweck und Inhalt von Musik: der Thesaurus ist da! 1982. *Forum Musikbibliothek* 3: 180-2. Translation: Occasion, purpose and content of music: The thesaurus is here!
643. Review. Bradley, C. J. Music collection in American libraries: A chronology. 1982. *Notes* 39: 357-58.
644. Bartis, P. T. 1982. "A history of the Archive of Folk Song at the Library of Congress: The first fifty years." University of Pennsylvania. Ph.D. thesis.
645. Dijk, W. and Van Hees, C. C. 1982. Enkele kanttekeningen bij de beschrijvings regels voor gedruke muziek. *Open* 14: 221-24.
646. Dowell, Arlene Taylor. 1982. *AACR2 headings: A five-year projection of their impact on catalogs.* Littleton, Colo.: Libraries Unlimited.
647. Griffin, Marie. 1982. The IJS jazz register and indexes: Jazz discography in the computer era. *Annual review of jazz studies* 1: 110-27.
648. Hassell, Robert Hanks. 1982. Revising the Dewey music schedules: Tradition vs. innovation. *Library resources & technical services* 26: 192-03.
649. Koltypina, Galina B. 1982. Standardization of the bibliographic description of printed music in the USSR. *Fontes artis musicae* 29: 47-48.
650. Lanzke, Heinz. 1982. Musiksonderregeln zu den Regeln für die alphabetische Katalogisierung. *Fontes artis musicae* 29: 49-51.
651. Lerch, Dieter. 1982. Maschinelle Erfassung und Erschliessung von Musikdaten. *Forum Musikbibliothek* 2: 65-90. Translation: Mechanized documentation and cataloguing of musical data.
652. Makela, Kyosti. 1982. Musiikiaineiston hakuelementit muotoutuvat. *Kirjastolehti* 75: 142-43.
653. Mayson, William Augustus. 1982. "Organizing the instrumental music ensemble library with the aid of a machine-assisted system." Ohio State University. D.M.A. thesis.
654. Miller, Karen and Miller, A. Patricia. 1982. Syncopation automation: An online thematic index. *Information technology and libraries* 1: 270-74.
655. Philp, Geraint J. 1982. The proposed revision of 780: Music and problems on the development of faceted classification for music. *Brio* 19: 1-13.

656. Plesske, Hans-Martin. 1982. Einige Bemerkungen zum EDV-Project Bibliographienherstellung der Deutschen Bücherei. *Fontes artis musicae* 29: 51-53. Translation: Some comments on the electronic data processing project for bibliographical production at the German Library.
657. Pratt, George. 1982. The user and the music library. *Brio* 19: 44-47.
658. Research Libraries Group, Inc. 1982. *Recordings field guide.* Stanford, Calif.: Research Libraries Group.
659. ———. 1982. *Scores field guide.* Stanford, Calif.: Research Libraries Group.
660. Richmond, S. 1982. Problems in applying AACR2 to music materials. *Library resources & technical services* 26: 204-11.
661. Rösner, Helmut. 1982. Stuttgarter Akzente. *Forum Musik-bibliothek* 4: 217-33. Translation: Aspects from Stuttgart. Report of 1982 conference of German section of International Association of Music Libraries.
662. Rogers, J. V. 1982. *Nonprint cataloging for multimedia collections; A guide based on AACR2.* Littleton, Colo.: Libraries Unlimited.
663. Schiodt, Nanna. 1982. Relationship of the IAML cataloguing code to the newly completed ISBD (PM and NBM) and AACR2: A preliminary study of the need and the feasibility of revising the IAML cataloguing code in the light of these developments. *Fontes artis musicae* 29: 54-56.
664. Seibert, Donald C. 1982. *The MARC format: From inception to publication.* Philadelphia: Music Library Association. MLA technical reports No. 13.
665. Sweeney, Russell. 1982. The proposed revision of 780 music: A reply. *Brio* 19: 47-49.
666. Tomaszewski, W. 1982. Polish work on the standard bibliographic description for printed music. *Fontes artis musicae* 29: 56-58.
667. Varga, Ildiko. 1982. Bibliographic description of sound records. *International cataloguing* 11: 7-8.
668. ———. 1982. Disk on the desk. *Fontes artis musicae* 29: 19.
669. Walcott, Ronald. 1982. American Folklife Center project: The federal cylinder project. *Phonographic bulletin* 33: 13-22.
670. Woakes, Harriet C. 1982. The sound archives of the Centre for Nigerian Cultural Studies. *Phonographic bulletin* 32: 15-23.
671. Youngholm, Philip. 1982. Foreign-language musical uniform titles required by AACR2. *Unabashed librarian* 43: 31-32.
672. Cataloguing Commission. 1983. *Fontes artis musicae* 30: 52-56.

Chronological Listing 73

673. Sound recording vendor offers MARC cataloging. 1983. *Library journal* 108: 2203.
674. Bowles, Garrett H. 1983. Cataloging 78-RPM recordings in the United States. *Brio* 20, no. 1: 8-10.
675. Carter, Nancy F. 1983. Sheet music cataloguing system for sound recordings. *Information technology and libraries* 2: 52-55.
676. Deathridge, J. 1983. Cataloguing Wagner. *Musical times* 124: 92-96.
677. Frost, Carolyn O. 1983. *Cataloging nonbook materials: Problems in theory and practice*. Littleton, Colo.: Libraries Unlimited.
678. Hardeck, Erwin. 1983. *Musikalien-Zentralkatalog und Musikalien-Leihverkehr: Planungsgutachten zur Einrichtung eines bundesweiten Leihverkehrs für Musikalien auf der Grundlage eines Musikalien-Zentralkatalogs der Musikbibliotheken der Bundesrepublik Deutschland*. West Germany: Deutsches Bibliotheksinstitut. Translation: Central catalog for music and music circulation: Plans for the establishment of a federal circulating library for music on the basis of a central catalog for the music libraries of the BRD.
679. Kaufman, Judith. 1983. *Library of Congress subject headings for recordings of Western non-classical music*. Philadelphia: Music Library Association. MLA technical reports, no. 14.
680. Petts, Leonard. 1983. *The story of "Nipper" and "His Master's Voice."* Bournemouth, England: Talking Machine Review. 2nd rev. ed.
681. Rosenberg, Kenyon Charles. 1983. Direct and digital sound recordings: Basics for librarians. *Library journal* 108: 879-80.
682. Smiraglia, Richard P. 1983. *Cataloging music: A manual for use with AACR2*. Lake Crystal, Minn.: Soldier Creek Press.
683. Wallon, Simone and Dorfmüller, Kurt. 1983. *Catalogage des enregistrements sonores*. Frankfurt; New York: C.F. Peters. Code international de catalogage de la musique v. 5. Translation: The cataloging of sound recordings.
684. Wursten, Richard Bruce. 1983. Music goes on-line: Retrospective conversion of card catalog records for music scores at Morris Library (SIU-C). *Illinois libraries*, 346-48.
685. Cundiff, Morgan. 1984. Computer-generated cataloging projects in the International Piano Archives at Maryland. *Phonographic bulletin* 38: 22-28.
686. Frisoli, Patrizia. 1984. Teatro e musica nel soggettario italiano. *Bollettino d'informazioni (Associazione Italiana Biblioteche)* 24: 197-200. Translation: Theater and music in Italian cataloging rules.

687. Gregor, Dorothy. 1984. *Retrospective conversion of music materials: Report of a meeting sponsored by the Council on Library Resources, July 18-19, 1984, Wayzata, Minnesota*. Washington, D.C.: Council on Library Resources. Bibliographic Service Development Program.
688. Held, Naomi Edwards. 1984. Another ample field: Music cataloging at the University of California, Berkeley. *Cum notis variorum* 83: 29-35, 48.
689. Weidow, Judy. 1984. *Music cataloging policy in the general libraries*. Austin: University of Texas. Contributions to librarianship no. 8.
690. Zanetti, Emilia. 1984. Musica nelle norme italiane di catalogazione. *Bollettino d'informazioni (Associazione Italiana Biblioteche)* 24: 173-8.
691. Zecca Laterza, Agostina. 1984. Classificazione e musica. DDC-proposed revision of 780, music. *Bollettino d'informazioni (Associazione Italiana Biblioteche)* 24: 179-84.
692. The national plan for retrospective conversion in music. 1985. *Library of Congress information bulletin* 44: 205-6.
693. Austin, Derek. 1985. *British catalogue of music: Code of practice for the application of PRECIS*. London: British Library, Bibliographic Services Division.
694. Bryant, Eric Thomas. 1985. *Music librarianship: A practical guide*. Metuchen, N.J.: Scarecrow Press. 2nd ed. with the assistance of Guy A. Marco.
695. Cody, Jan. 1985. Review. Gregor, Dorothy, ed. *Retrospective conversion of music materials*. *Notes* 42: 298-9.
696. Dowell, Arlene Taylor. 1985. Review. Smiraglia, Richard P. *Cataloging music*. *Cataloging & classification quarterly* 5: 90-91.
697. Gabbard, Páula Beversdorf. 1985. LCSH and PRECIS in music: A comparison. *Library quarterly* 55: 192-206.
698. Minarek, Erwin. 1985. Bochumer ADV-Klassifikation für Musikalien. Möglichkeiten der mehrdimensionalen Sacherschliessung. *Forum Musikbibliothek* 1: 21-43. Translation: The Bochum electronic data processing classification for music: The possiblities of multi-dimensional subject cataloguing.
699. Papakhian, Arsen Ralph. 1985. The frequency of personal name headings in the Indiana University Music Library card catalogs. *Library resources & technical services* 29: 273-85.

700. Price, Harry Howe. 1985. Subject access to jazz and popular music materials on Library of Congress catalog records. *Fontes artis musicae* 32: 42-54.
701. Shaw, Sarah J. and Shiere, Lauralee. 1985. *Sheet music cataloging and processing: A manual*. Canton, Mass.: Music Library Association. MLA technical reports no. 15.
702. Smiraglia, Richard P. 1985. Theoretical considerations in the bibliographic control of music materials in libraries. *Cataloging & classification quarterly* 5: 1-16.
703. Bradley, Carol June. 1986. Notes of some pioneers: America's first music librarians. *Notes* 43: 272-91.
704. Colby, Michael D. 1986. Review. Shaw, Sarah J. *Sheet music cataloging and processing*. *Notes* 42: 779-80.
705. Davidson, Mary Wallace. 1986. Towards a national program for the retrospective conversion of music records, presented at the 1985 IAML conference. *Fontes artis musicae* 33: 52-9.
706. Famera, Karen M. 1986. Review. Kaufman, Judith. *Library of Congress subject headings for recordings of Western non-classical music*. *Sonneck Society Newsletter, USA* 12, no. 1: 29-30.
707. Gemert, Joost van. 1986. The co-operative "Muziek Catalogus Nederland." *Fontes artis musicae* 33: 280-4.
708. McClymonds, Marita P. and Walker, Diane Parr. 1986. U.S. RISM libretto project with guidelines for cataloguing in the MARC format. *Notes* 43: 19-35.
709. Online Computer Library Center, Inc. 1986. *Scores format*. Dublin, Ohio: OCLC.
710. ———. 1986. *Sound recordings format*. Dublin, Ohio: OCLC.
711. Poroila, Heikki. 1986. Säännöistä yhtenäiseen käytäntöön. *Kirjastolehti* 79: 346-8.
712. Sarno, Jania. 1986. Nuevas normas para la catalogación de los manuscritos musicales: Una propuesta italiana. *Brussels Museum of Musical Instruments Bulletin*: 83-88. Translation: New rules for cataloging music manuscripts: an Italian proposal.
713. Seibert, Donald C. and Herrold, Charles M., Jr. 1986. Uniform titles for music under AACR2 and its predecessors: The problems and possibilities of developing a user-friendly repertoire. *Cataloguing special materials: Critiques and innovations*, 133-50. Phoenix: Oryx Press.
714. Smiraglia, Richard P. 1986. *Cataloging music: A manual for use with AACR2*. Lake Crystal, Minn.: Soldier Creek Press. 2nd ed.

715. Thompson, Annie F. 1986. Music cataloging in academic libraries and the case for physical decentralization: A survey. *Journal of academic librarianship* 12: 79-83.
716. Woakes, Harriet C. 1986. The development of a classification for non-Western music: A modification of Library of Congress class M. *Library focus* 4, no. 1-2: 105-25.
717. Young, James Bradford. 1986. A comparison of PRECIS and Library of Congress subject headings for the retrieval of printed music. Research paper, University of Illinois.
718. Music libraries cooperate on retro conversion project. 1987. *Library journal* 112: 123.
719. Anderson, James D. 1987. Review. Smiraglia, Richard P. *Cataloging music. Library journal* 112: 56.
720. Bielska, Krystyna. 1987. ISBD for sound recordings in Poland, paper given at IAML Congress in Stockholm, August 1986. *Fontes artis musicae* 34: 138-42.
721. Bratcher, Perry. 1987. Music OCLC recon: The practical approach. *Cataloging & classification quarterly* 8, no. 2: 41-8.
722. Garland, Catherine. 1987. PREMARC: Retrospective conversion at the Library of Congress, paper given at the IAML Congress in Stockholm, August 1986. *Fontes artis musicae* 34: 132-8.
723. Hardeck, Erwin. 1987. Verbundkatalogisierung für Musikalien? *Forum Musikbibliothek*, no. 4: 198-208. Translation: Joint cataloging for music materials?
724. Olsen, Vivian. 1987. Three research libraries convert music materials. *Research libraries in OCLC*, no. 23: 1-7.
725. Smith, Ruth S. 1987. Cataloging sound recordings. *Cataloging made easy: How to organize your congregation's library.* New York: Seabury Press. Rev. ed.
726. Tolstrup, Kamma. 1987. Music cataloguing: Printed music and sound recordings, paper presented at the annual seminar of the LA Cataloguing and Indexing Group, April 1986. *Catalogue & index* 84/5: 7-9.
727. Turner, Malcolm. 1987. Some current developments in the bibliographic control of music and the British Library's catalogues. *International cataloguing* 16: 35-6.
728. Bratcher, Perry. 1988. *Music subject headings.* Lake Crystal, Minn.: Soldier Creek Press.
729. Carter, Nancy F. 1988. Enhancing nonbook cataloging for online catalogs, use of contents notes for music cataloging. *Technicalities* 8, March: 8-9.

Chronological Listing 77

730. Chailley, Marie-Noëlle. 1988. Proposition de classification décimale pour les besoins des bibliothéques musicales de type multimedia. *Fontes artis musicae* 35: 243-56.
731. Davidson, Mary Wallace. 1988. Review. Smiraglia, Richard P. Cataloging music. *Library resources & technical services* 32: 90-92.
732. Drone, Jeanette. 1988. *Music subject headings from the machine-readable Library of Congress subject authority file.* Dublin, Ohio: OCLC Online Computer Library Center Inc., Office for Research. Research report series, no. 88: 4-5.
733. Erdelyi, Frigyesne. 1988. Flexibilis zenei osztalyozasi rendszer: Keigeszitesi javaslatok az apparatus jelzetelesehez. *Konyvtari-Figyelo* 34, no. 1: 50-67. Translation: Flexible music classification scheme: Suggestions for the extension of the codes of the scheme.
734. Fulton, Gloria. 1988. MUSCAT: A music cataloging inquiry system from California, paper presented at SCIL '88. *Library software review* 7: 192.
735. Hell, Helmut. 1988. Musikalien im Schlagwortkatalog. *Forum Musikbibliothek*, no. 3: 185-201. Translation: Music in the subject-headings catalog.
736. High, Walter M. 1988. Review. Almquist, Sharon G. *Sound recordings and the library. Cataloging & classification quarterly* 1: 150-1.
737. Hirao, Kozo. 1988. The descriptive cataloguing of music in Japan. *Fontes artis musicae* 35: 80-83.
738. Holzberlein, Deanne and Jones, Dolly. 1988. *Cataloging sound recordings: A manual with examples.* New York: Haworth Press. Monographic supplement to *Cataloging & classification quarterly*, no. 1.
739. Kranz, Jack. 1988. The music uniform title: Sources for the novice cataloger, AACR2 chapter 25 rules. *Cataloging & classification quarterly* 9, no. 2: 73-80.
740. Lönn, Anders. 1988. Thematic catalogue numbers in music uniform titles: An international comparison. *Fontes artis musicae* 35: 224-43.
741. McKnight, Mark. 1988. Cataloging local popular sound recordings. *Louisiana Library Association bulletin* 51: 71-5.
742. ———. 1988. Improving access to music: A report of the MLA Music Thesaurus Project Working Group. *Notes* 45: 714-21.

743. Müller-Benedict, Markus. 1988. Populärmusik in der Musikalien-Freihandsystematik—Ein Konzept. *Forum Musikbibliothek* 2: 95-120. Translation: Classification of popular music for open-stack collections: A proposal.
744. Stephens, Norris L. 1988. Review. Smiraglia, Richard P. *Cataloging music. Cataloging & classification quarterly* 9, no. 1: 129-30.
745. Turner, Malcolm. 1988. A suggested list of thematic catalogues and their recommended abbreviations. *Brio* 25: 25-30.
746. Weitz, Jay. 1988. More news from OCLC. *Music OCLC Users Group newsletter* 34: 5.
747. *Authority control in music libraries.* 1989. Canton, Mass.: Music Library Association. Proceedings of the Music Library Association preconference, March 5, 1985.
748. Coral, Lenore. 1989. The ISBD (NBM) revision: An historical review, especially as it describes sound recordings; presented at the 1988 IAML conference. *Fontes artis musicae* 36: 55-7.
749. Daub, Peggy Ellen. 1989. Review. Smiraglia, Richard P. *Cataloging music. Journal of academic librarianship* 14: 375.
750. Perry, Helga. 1989. Musical bumps: Indexing musical terms. *Indexer* 16, no. 4: 251-53.
751. Schultz, Lois S. 1989. Designing an expert system to assign Dewey classification numbers to scores. *National online meeting proceedings 1989, New York 9-11 May*, ed. Nixon, C. and Padgett, L., 393-97. Medford, N.J.: Learned Information.
752. Smiraglia, Richard P. 1989. *Music cataloging: The bibliographic control of printed and recorded music in libraries.* Littleton, Colo.: Libraries Unlimited.
753. ―――. 1989. Uniform titles for music: An exercise in collocating works. *Cataloging & classification quarterly* 9, no. 3: 97-114.
754. Tucker, Ruth W. 1989. Music retrospective conversion at the University of California at Berkeley; conversion of musical scores through a consortium; presented at the 1988 ALA Conference. *Technical services quarterly* 7, no. 2: 13-28.
755. Turner, Malcolm. 1989. Waving or drowning? The growth of the music catalogues in the British Library. *Fontes artis musicae* 36: 297-304.
756. Young, Percy. 1989. Of music and indexing. *Indexer* 16: 177-80.
757. Aurelle, Elisabeth. 1990. Review. *Authority control in music libraries. Notes* 47: 409-10.

Chronological Listing

758. Barnhart, Linda K. 1990. Review. Bratcher, P. and Smith, J. *Music subject headings. Cataloging & classification quarterly* 11, no. 2: 115-17.
759. ———. 1990. Review. Smiraglia, Richard P. *Cataloging music. Cataloging & classification quarterly* 11, no. 2: 118-19.
760. ———. 1990. Review. Smiraglia, Richard P. *Music cataloging. Notes* 47: 410-412.
761. Cobbe, Hugh. 1990. "Jam tomorrow": The present and future state of the British Library's automated music catalogues part 2. *Fontes artis musicae* 37: 53-56.
762. Damiani, Maria Raffaella. 1990. "Norme di catalogazione della musica a stampa: Una panoramica internazionale." U. degli Studi di Pavia, Scuola di Paleografia e Filologia Musicale. Tesi di laurea. Translation: Cataloguing standards of printed music: An international overview.
763. Davidson, Mary Wallace. 1990. Review. Smiraglia, Richard P. *Music cataloging* 2d ed. *Library resources & technical services* 34: 411-12.
764. Hoban, Michi S. 1990. Sound recording cataloging: A practical approach: Cataloging compact disc recordings issued previously in LP or cassette format; experience of Dartmouth College Library. *Cataloging & classification quarterly* 12, no. 2: 3-26.
765. Kranz, Jack. 1990. Paraprofessional involvement in music cataloging: A case study in the University Libraries at California State University, Northridge with OCLC member-input copy. *Cataloging & classification quarterly* 10, no. 4: 89-98.
766. Schuursma, Ann. 1990. Summary report of activities: IAML Project Group on Classification & Indexing. *Fontes artis musicae* 37: 46-8.
767. Stephens, Norris L. 1990. Review. Smiraglia, Richard P. *Music cataloging. Cataloging & classification quarterly* 12, no. 1: 117-18.
768. Thomas, David H. 1990. Cataloging sound recordings using archival methods. *Cataloging & classification quarterly* 11, nos. 3/4: 193-212.
769. Turner, Malcolm. 1990. "Jam tomorrow": The present and future state of the British Library's automated music catalogues part 1. *Fontes artis musicae* 37: 48-52.
770. Usher, Caroline Payson. 1990. "Cataloging musical iconography: The Répertoire internationale d'iconographie musicale." University of North Carolina, Chapel Hill. M. L. S. thesis.

771. Voedisch, Virginia G. 1990. Don't knock it 'til you try it—OCLC recently released two CD-ROM music databases: the Music Library and the Music Cataloging Collection. *OCLC micro* 6: 2-4.
772. Weitz, Jay. 1990. *Music coding and tagging.* Lake Crystal, Minn.: Soldier Creek Press.
773. Wursten, Richard Bruce. 1990. In celebration of Revised 780: Music in the Dewey decimal classification ed. 20. Canton, Mass.: Music Library Association.
774. Allan, Ann G. and Park, Amey L. 1991. *AACR 2* revised—an update for public service librarians: Improvements that affect the cataloging of sound recordings, computer files, and materials for the visually impaired. *Public libraries* 30: 101-5.
775. Borghi, Renato and Guerrini, Mauro. 1991. Descrizione della musica a stampa fra ISBD (PM), AACR2 e AACR2 R. *Bollettino d'informazioni (Associazione Italiana Biblioteche)* 31: 1-19. Translation: Description of printed music using ISBD (PM), AACR2 and AACR2 R.
776. Burbank, Richard. 1991. Review. *Authority control in music libraries. Library resources & technical services* 35: 125.
777. Burbank, Richard. 1991. Review. Smiraglia, R. P. *Music cataloging. Fontes artis musicae* 38: 76-7.
778. Burbank, Richard. 1991. Review. Weitz, Jay. *Music coding & tagging. Library resources & technical services* 35: 234-5.
779. Colby, Michael D. 1991. Review. Wursten, R. B. *In celebration of Revised 780. Notes* 47: 1178-79.
780. Crow, Linda. 1991. Shelf arrangement systems for sound recordings: Survey of American academic music libraries. *Technical services quarterly* 8, no. 4: 1-24.
781. Davis, Deta S. 1991. Recent changes in computer and electronic music subject headings at the Library of Congress. *Proceedings: International Computer Music Conference, Montreal, 1991,* 495-500. Montreal: McGill University.
782. Harrold, Ann and Lea, Graham. 1991. *Musaurus: A music thesaurus.* London: Music Press.
783. Herrold, Charles M. 1991. Review. Weitz, Jay. *Music coding & tagging. Cataloging & classification quarterly* 13, no. 2: 122-3.
784. Price, Harry Howe. 1991. Review. Bratcher, P. and Smith, J. *Music subject headings. Notes* 47: 1179-81.
785. Price, Harry Howe. 1991. Review. Drone, Jeannette. *Music subject headings from the machine-readable Library of Congress subject authority file. Notes* 47: 1179-81.

786. Price, Harry Howe. 1991. Review. Weitz, Jay. *Music coding & tagging. Notes* 47: 1181.
787. Redfern, Brian L. 1991. On first looking into Dewey decimal classification 20, class 780, a review article. *Brio* 28: 19-28.
788. Segura Aguilo, Joan. 1991. Catalogació de manuscrits musicals. *Estudis Balearics* 39: 75-76. Translation: Cataloguing of music manuscripts.
789. Sommerfield, David. 1991. Review. Wursten, R. B. *In celebration of Revised 780. Library resources & technical services* 35: 340.
790. Thomas, Alan R. 1991. Review. Weitz, Jay. *Music coding & tagging. Library Association record* 93: 405.
791. Wursten, Richard Bruce. 1991. Review. *DDC, Dewey decimal classification. Notes* 48: 143-5.
792. Stauffer, Suzanne M. 1991-1992. Subject headings for Jewish liturgical sheet music used at Hebrew Union College. *Judaica librarianship* 6: 94-104.
793. Bauer, Gerd. 1992. Review. Harrold, Ann and Lea, Graham. *Musaurus: A music thesaurus. International classification* 19: 39.
794. Burbank, Richard and Henigman, Barbara D. 1992. Music symbols and online catalogs: A survey of vendors and an assessment of retrieval capabilities. *Information technology and libraries* 11: 203-9.
795. Gross, Linda. 1992. Heartaches by the number: Cataloging country music at the Country Music Foundation Library. *North Carolina libraries* 50: 198-200.
796. Harperink, Bernadette. 1992. Bladmuziek: bijzonder bibliotheekmateriaal? *Open* 24: 428-32. Translation: Sheet music: A special item in the library?
797. Hell, Helmut. 1992. Sonderregeln für Musikdrücke und Musiktonträger zu den Regeln für den Schlagwortkatalog (RSWK). *Fontes artis musicae* 39: 179-85. Translation: Rules for printed music and sound recordings in a subject catalog.
798. Hemmasi, Harriette. 1992. ARIS (Anderson Rowley information systems) music thesaurus: Another view of LCSH. *Library resources & technical services* 36: 487-503.
799. Koth, Michelle and Green, Laura Gayle. 1992. Workflow considerations in retrospective conversion projects for scores; case studies from seven academic music libraries: Presented at a Music OCLC Users Group meeting, Tucson, Ariz., February 1990. *Cataloging & classification quarterly* 14, no. 3/4: 75-102.

800. Leazer, Gregory H. 1992. The effectiveness of keyword searching in the retrieval of musical works on sound recordings, OPAC retrieval techniques. *Cataloging & classification quarterly* 15, no. 3: 15-55.
801. Müller-Benedict, Markus. 1992. Klassifikatorische Inhaltserschliessung im Fachgebiet Musik. *Fontes artis musicae* 39: 185-8. Translation: Development of a music classification scheme.
802. Runchok, Rita and Droste, Kathleen. 1992. *Class M, music and books on music (combined schedule through 1991): Library of Congress classification schedules combined with additions and changes through 1991.* Washington, D.C.: Library of Congress. Subject Cataloging Division. Gale Research.
803. Studwell, William E. and Ericksen, Dawn A. 1992. Music libraries and a subject heading code. *Music reference services quarterly* 1, no. 1: 73-75.
804. Troutman, Leslie A. 1992. The online public access catalog and music materials: Issues for system and interface design (ILLINET Online at the University of Illinois at Urbana-Champaign). *Advances in online public access catalogs*, 9-37. Vol. 1. Meckler.
805. Weiland, Sue. 1992. Music scores: Retroconversion or recataloging? at Wichita State University Music Library. *Technical services quarterly* 10, no. 1: 61-71.
806. Bratcher, Perry. 1993. Cataloguing music: The non-musician's perspective. *Music reference services quarterly* 1, no. 3: 65-77.
807. Bucknum, Mary Russell. 1993. Cataloging field recordings of American Indian languages at Indiana University, Bloomington. *Cataloging & classification quarterly* 17: 15-27.
808. Gottlieb, Jane. 1993. Sharing information on archival collections: MARC AMC and beyond in the U.S. experience of the Juilliard School and 12 other institutions. *Fontes artis musicae* 40: 228-38.
809. Massip, Catherine. 1993. Documents musicaux. *Bulletin des bibliothèques de France* 38, no. 5: 57-59. Translation: Cataloging music literature.
810. Miura, H. 1993. Critical essays on Nippon decimal classification, proposed 9th edition "Arts class." *Toshokan Kai* 44, no. 5: 230-35.
811. Roth, Christine. 1993. Musique dans SIBIL—Lausanne integrated library system. *Fontes artis musicae* 40: 207-27.

Chronological Listing 83

812. Runchok, Rita and Droste, Kathleen. 1993. *Class M, music and books on music. Library of Congress classification schedules: A cumulation of additions and changes through 1992.* Washington, D.C.: Library of Congress. Subject Cataloging Division. Gale Research, 3rd ed.
813. Cassaro, James P. 1994. Music cataloguing and the future. *Fontes artis musicae* 41, no. 245-50.
814. Elliker, Calvin. 1994. Classification schemes for scores: Analysis of structural levels. *Notes* 50: 1269-320.
815. Gaschignard, Jean-Paul. 1994. Trois sources pour les notices de documents sonores. *Bulletin d'informations de l'Association des bibliothècaires français* 163: 81.
816. Hartsock, Ralph. 1994. *Notes for music catalogers: Examples illustrating AACR2 in the online bibliographic record.* Lake Crystal, Minn.: Soldier Creek Press.
817. Hemmasi, Harriette. 1994. The music thesaurus: Functions and foundations. *Notes* 50: 875-82.
818. MacLeod, Judy and Lloyd, Kim. 1994. A study of music cataloging backlogs: Survey of 357 institutional subscribers to the *Music cataloging bulletin. Library resources & technical services* 38: 7-15.
819. Mantz, Stephen Lee. 1994. "An examination of the music headings in the Library of Congress subject headings." University of North Carolina, Chapel Hill. M. L. S. thesis.
820. Massip, Catherine. 1994. Musique imprimée. *Bulletin d'informations de l'Association des bibliothècaires français*, no. 163: 87-8. Translation: Printed music.
821. Parmentier, Martine and Raccah, Philippe. 1994. Entre silence et cacophonie: Le catalogage informatisé des phonogrammes. *Bulletin d'informations de l'Association des bibliothècaires français,* no.163: 79-80. Translation: Between silence and cacophony: Computerized cataloging of sound recordings.
822. Runchok, Rita and Droste, Kathleen. 1994. *Class M: Music and books on music. SuperLCCS: Gale's Library of Congress classification schedules combined with additions and changes through 1993.* Washington, D.C.: Library of Congress. Subject Cataloging Division. Gale Research, 3rd ed.
823. Witten, Jane Daley. 1994. "Providing access to a collection of recorded music at the University of North Carolina at Chapel Hill's student radio station, WXYC-FM." University of North Carolina, Chapel Hill. M.L.S. thesis.

824. Hemmasi, Harriette. 1995. The music thesaurus project at Rutgers University. *New Jersey libraries* 28, no. 2: 21-23.
825. Inman, Ruth A. 1995. Are Title II-C grants worth it? The effects of the Associated Music Library Group's retrospective conversion project at the University of Illinois at Chicago. *Library resources & technical services* 39: 167-76.
826. Meyers, J. A. 1995. Music: Special characteristics for indexing and cataloguing. *Indexer* 19, no. 4: 269-74.
827. Poroila, Heikki. 1995. Hankalat musiikkinimet: Ohjeluettelo musikin luetteloinnissa ja tiedonhaussa käytettävistä nimimuodoista. *Suomen Musiikkikirjastoyhdistyksen Julkaisusarja* 20. Translation: Difficult musical titles: A guide for music cataloging and information retrieval.
828. Tanabe, Hisayuki. 1995. Wagakuni ni okeru shichokaku shiryo soshikika no shiteki kosatsu. *Tokoha Gakuen Tanki Daigaku Kiyo* 26: 257-72. Translation: A historical approach to cataloging and classification of music and sound recordings for libraries in Japan.
829. Working Group on the Core Bibliographic Record for Music and Sound Recordings—appointed at the 1994 IAML Conference. 1996. *Fontes artis musicae* 43: 208-9.
830. Barriault, Jeannine and Jean, Stéphane. 1996. La description des archives de musique: Un exemple Canadien—Music Division of the National Library of Canada. *Fontes artis musicae* 43: 274-85. Translation: The description of music archives: A Canadian example.
831. Bauman, Joanne. 1996. Sound librarian—The music cataloging tool for Windows. *American record guide* 59, no. 5: 284.
832. Garrison, Ellen. 1996. Neither fish nor fowl nor good red meat: Using archival descriptive techniques for special format materials—experience of the Center for Popular Music at Middle Tennessee State University. *Archival issues* 21, no. 1: 61-71.
833. Hardeck, Erwin. 1996. Revision RAK-Musik: Abschlußbericht. *Forum Musikbibliothek*, no. 2: 110-23. Translation: RAK-Musik revision: Final report.
834. MacNeil, Heather. 1996. Subject access to archival fonds: Balancing provenance and pertinence. *Fontes artis musicae* 43: 242-58.
835. McKee, Elwood A. 1996. Cataloging system review. *ARSC journal* 27: 59-64.
836. ———. 1996. Developing and selecting cataloging systems for private collections. *ARSC journal* 27: 53-58.

Chronological Listing

837. Riva, Federica. 1996. E dopo Sartori? Considerazioni sulla catalogazione dei libretti. *Rivista italiana di musicologia* 31: 91-118. Translation: And after Sartori? Remarks on the cataloging of librettos.
838. Schneider, Klaus. 1996. Über den Musik-Thesaurus und die inhaltliche Erschließung von Musik. *Forum Musikbibliothek*, no. Issue 2: 100-08. Translation: Concerning the musik thesaurus and content searching of music.
839. Bauman, Joanne. 1997. Review. *Classicat for Windows. American record guide* 60, no. 4: 251-53.
840. Cato, Anders. 1997. Working groups: core bibliographic record for music and sound recordings—report from the 1996 IAML Conference. *Fontes artis musicae* 44: 188.
841. Hieb, Fern. 1997. Issues in retrospective conversion for a small special collection: a case study, Moravian Music Foundation. *North Carolina Libraries* 55: 86-9.
842. McCleskey, Sarah E. 1997. "Access to popular song titles in the University of North Carolina at Chapel Hill Music Library." University of North Carolina, Chapel Hill. M. L. S. thesis.
843. Pavlovsky, Taras. 1997. Slavic sacred music: issues in cataloguing—paper presented at the 1997 MLA Conference. *Fontes artis musicae* 44: 248-65.
844. Smiraglia, Richard P. 1997. *Describing music materials: A manual for descriptive cataloging of printed and recorded music, music videos, and archival music collections, for use with AACR2 and APPM.* Lake Crystal, Minn.: Soldier Creek Press. 3rd ed., rev. and enl. Taras Pavlovsky.
845. Vellucci, Sherry L. 1997. *Bibliographic relationships in music catalogs*. Lanham, Md.: Scarecrow Press.
846. The core bibliographic record for music and sound recordings—working group report from the 1997 IAML Conference. 1998. *Fontes artis musicae* 45: 139-51.
847. Cassaro, James P. 1998. Subject Commission on Cataloguing. *Fontes artis musicae* 45: 165.
848. Colby, Michael D. 1998. Nailing Jell-o to a tree: Improving access to 20th-century music. *Cataloging & classification quarterly* 26, no. 3: 31-9.
849. Ezquerro Esteban, Antonio. 1998. Cataloguing musical sources in Spain: A RISM perspective. *Fontes artis musicae* 45: 81-9.
850. Hemmasi, Harriette. 1998. *Music subject headings*. Lake Crystal, Minn.: Soldier Creek Press.

851. Kuyper-Rushing, Lois. 1998. Review. Smiraglia, R. P. and Pavlovsky, T. Describing music materials. *Cataloging & classification quarterly* 26: 79-83.
852. Rogers, Carolyn, Gié, Hélène, and Brun, Corinne. 1998. Nouveau systeme de description instrumentale et vocale pour le catalogagedes partitions—reprinted from Ecouter-Voir. *Documentaliste* 35, no. 2: 101-5. Translation: A new system for instrumental and vocal description in a sheet music catalog.
853. Scharff, Mark. 1998. Review. Smiraglia, Richard P. *Describing music materials*. *Notes* 55: 379-81.
854. Thomas, David H. and Smiraglia, Richard P. 1998. Beyond the score. *Notes* 54: 649-66.
855. Vellucci, Sherry L. 1998. Bibliographic relationships and the future of music catalogues: Study at Sibley Music Library; revision of a paper presented at the 1997 IAML Conference. *Fontes artis musicae* 45: 213-26.
856. Wojnowska, Elzbieta. 1998. Probleme bei der Katalogisierung alter Musikdrücke im Lichte der Formate RISM und US-MARC. *Forum Musikbibliothek* 1: 61-66. Translation: Problems in cataloging old music editions in light of the RISM and U.S. MARC formats.
857. Barnhart, Linda K. 1999. Review. Vellucci, S. *Bibliographic relationships in music catalogs*. *Notes* 56: 111-13.
858. Elliker, Calvin. 1999. Toward a definition of sheet music. *Notes* 55: 835-59.
859. Koonce, Taneya Yvette. 1999. "Indexing rap music literature: An experiment into the creation of a rap music database using *The source: The magazine of hip-hop music, culture, and politics*." University of North Carolina at Chapel Hill. M. S. L. S. thesis.
860. Luttman, Stephen F. 1999. Good enough for jazz; or, Successful music cataloging for non-musicians. *Colorado libraries* 25, no. 2: 48-9.
861. Shanton, Kristina. 1999. Review. Hemmasi, H. and Rowley, F. *Music subject headings*. *Fontes artis musicae* 46: 356-7.
862. Vellucci, Sherry L. 1999. Metadata for music: Issues and directions. *Fontes artis musicae* 46: 205-17.
863. Winke, R. Conrad. 1999. Review. Hemmasi, H. and Rowley, F. *Music subject headings*. *Technicalities* 19, no. 2: 14-15.
864. Barnhart, Linda K. 2000. Review. Hemmasi, H. and Rowley, F. *Music subject headings*. *Notes* 56: 701-2.
865. Bauman, Joanne. 2000. Review. *ClassiCat version 2—Record cataloging software*. *American record guide* 63, no. 2: 300.

866. Hemmasi, Harriette and Young, James Bradford. 2000. LCSH for music: Historical and empirical perspectives. *Cataloging & classification quarterly* 29, nos. 1/2: 135-57.
867. Krummel, Donald W. 2000. On degressive music bibliography. *Notes* 56: 867-78.
868. Mudge, Suzanne and Hoek, D. J. 2000. Describing jazz, blues, and popular 78 RPM sound recordings: Suggestions and guidelines at Indiana University, Bloomington. *Cataloging & classification quarterly* 29, no. 3: 21-48.
869. Papakhian, Arsen Ralph. 2000. Music librarianship at the turn of the century: Cataloging. *Notes* 56: 581-90.

870. Brooklyn Public Library. n.d. *Music literature and scores together, expanded and modified from Dewey 780*.
871. Buenos Aires Biblioteca Nacional. n.d. *Classification de las obras de musica*.
872. Chicago Public Library. n.d. *Classification for music scores used in the Chicago Public Library*.
873. Cleveland Public Library. n.d. *Music classification*.
874. Greensboro, N.C. Public Schools. n.d. *Quick reference classification code for non-music records; for music records*. 7th ed., abridged.
875. Harvard Musical Association Library. n.d. *Classification of literature: Classification of music*.
876. Johansson, Corry. n.d. *ARAL: A coordination system of classification*. Stockholm: Swedish Broadcasting Corp., New Information Service.
877. Free Library of Philadelphia Music Dept. n.d. *Chamber music classification scheme: Modification of Altmann's Kammermusik Katalog (1931)*. Philadelphia: The Free Library. Adapted by E. R. Hartman.
878. Pittsburgh Public Schools. n.d. *Outline of classification for recordings, transcriptions and types*. Pittsburgh, Pa.
879. Radcliffe College Library. n.d. *Music classification. Literature of music. Collections of music; Scores of individual composers*. Cambridge, Mass.: Radcliffe College.
880. Toledo Public Library. n.d. *Music classification used at Toledo*. Toledo, Ohio: The Library.

Title Index

78 rpm phonorecords in the Jazz Archive, *445*

The AAA project, *533*

AACR, 1967: Chapters 13 & 14: A music librarian's view of a cataloguing code, *426*

AACR 2 revised—an update for public service librarians; improvements that affect the cataloging of sound recordings, computer files, and materials for the visually impaired, *774*

AACR2 and its implications for music cataloguing, *578*

AACR2 *headings: A five-year projection of their impact on catalogs,* *646*

AACR2: The first year at Urbana, *635*

Abstracts (of some recent articles on gramophone record libraries), *242*

Academic libraries using the LC classification system, *343*

Access to popular song titles in the University of North Carolina at Chapel Hill Music Library, *842*

Advances in librarianship v. 11, *640*

Advances in online public access catalogs, 804

The advantages of disorder, *512*

African music research transcription library of gramaphone records: Handbook for librarians, 83

ALA catalog rules: Author and title entries, 53

All on the card: Sullivan Memorial Library has record cataloging plan, *69*

American Folklife Center project: The Federal Cylinder Project, *669*

American music catalogs, *11*

American music libraries and librarianship: An overview in the eighties, *641*
And what is musicology?, *405*
Anglo-American cataloging rules, *352*
Anglo-American cataloging rules: Chapter 14 revised: Sound recordings, *507*
Anlass, Zweck und Inhalt av Musikalier, *642*
Another ample field: Music cataloging at the University of California, Berkeley, *688*
ANSCR: The alpha-numeric system for classification of recordings, *401*
Anweisung zur Titelaufnahme von Musikalien, *38*
APPARAT: A computer cataloguing system for sound recordings, *591*
ARAL: A coordination system of classification, *876*
Are Title II-C grants worth it? The effects of the Associated Music Library Group's retrospective conversion project at the University of Illinois at Chicago, *825*
ARIS (Anderson Rowley information systems) music thesaurus: Another view of LCSH, *798*
Arrangement and classification of sound recordings, *572*
Att katalogisera skivor, *540*
Auckland University Library, *79*
Audio, *546*
Audio, etc., *567*
Audio-visual aids and the college library, *59*
Audio-visual aids and the library, *45*
Audio-visual materials, *241*
Audio-visual materials in the library, *151*
Aufbau und Verwendungsmöglichkeiten einer Discothek wertvoller Gesangsaufnahmen im Sendebetrieb, *148*
Authority control in music libraries, *747*
Automated bibliographic control of music, *615*
Automated music, *529*
Automation and music cataloging, *386*
The automation plans of the music library of the Nederlandse Omroep Stichting—Dutch Broadcasting Foundation, *541*
Autoren-Katalog der Musikdrücke, *161*
Auxiliary catalogues in the music library, *200*

BBC Gramophone Library cataloguing practice, *417*
Beyond the score, *854*
Bibliografischeskoe opisanie notnykg izdanii, *625*

Bibliographic control of audio-visual materials: Report of a special committee, *164*
Bibliographic control of nonprint media, 452
Bibliographic control of printed music, *562*
Bibliographic description of sound records, *667*
Bibliographic relationships and the future of music catalogues: Study at Sibley Music Library: Revision of a paper presented at the 1997 IAML Conference, *855*
Bibliographic relationships in music catalogs, 845
Bladmuziek: Bijzonder bibliotheekmateriaal?, *796*
Bochumer ADV-Klassifikation für Musikalien. Möglichkeiten der mehrdimensionalen Sacherschliessung, *698*
The British catalogue of music classification, 209
British catalogue of music: Code of practice for the application of PRECIS, 693
British Library: Pilot experiment on a national cataloguing service for non-book materials, *528*

C.U. classification for phonorecords, 270
A card index for your records, *128*
Care and treatment of music in a library, 21
Cartographic materials, manuscripts, music, and sound recordings, *598*
Catalog of music collection, *27*
Catalogación y clasificación de musica, *125*
Catalogación y Classificación de la musica cubana, 279
Catalogació de manuscrits musicals, *788*
Catalogage des documents ethnomusico-logiques sonores (disques et bandes) de l'Institute de musicologie de Paris, *248*
Catalogage des enregistrements sonores, 683
Cataloging 78-RPM recordings in the United States, *674*
Cataloging and classification of music on phonorecords: Some considerations, *483*
Cataloging and classification of phonograph records, *213*
Cataloging and filing of phonograph records, *34*
Cataloging and the computer, *451*
Cataloging field recordings of American Indian languages at Indiana University, Bloomington, *807*
Cataloging local popular sound recordings, *741*
Cataloging made easy: How to organize your congregation's library, 557, 725
Cataloging music: A manual for use with AACR2, 682, 714

Cataloging musical iconography: The Répertoire internationale d'iconographie musicale, *770*
Cataloging non-book materials, *77*
Cataloging nonbook materials: Problems in theory and practice, 677
Cataloging of audiovisual materials: A manual based on AACR2, 630
Cataloging of "folk music" on records, *188*
The cataloging of folk-song records, *35*
Cataloging of music and records, *170*
Cataloging of music in the Seattle Public Library, *12*
The cataloging of music in the visual arts, *132*
Cataloging of phonograph records, *114*
Cataloging of phonorecords, *494*
Cataloging of records, *202, 210, 211*
The cataloging of records, musical and non-musical, for a general library, *62*
Cataloging phonograph records for the veterans hospitals, *75*
Cataloging phonorecordings: Problems and possibilities, 495
Cataloging recordings, *298*
Cataloging recordings in the Illinois State Library, *127*
Cataloging sound recordings, *557, 725*
Cataloging sound recordings: A manual with examples, 738
Cataloging sound recordings using archival methods, *768*
Cataloging system review, *835*
Cataloging the contents of certain recordings, *316*
Cataloging the music library, *441*
Cataloging the non-musical phonograph record, *67*
Cataloging the record collection in McMaster University Library, *63*
Cataloging the small music collection, *18*
Cataloging with copy: A decision-maker's handbook, 513
The cataloguing, arrangement and filing of serial materials in special libraries, 80
Cataloguing commission, *672*
Cataloguing music and records in the Douglas Library, *66*
Cataloguing music: The non-musician's perspective, *806*
Cataloguing musical sources in Spain: A RISM perspective, *849*
Cataloguing of gramophone records, *197*
Cataloguing of music, *1, 37, 392*
Cataloguing special materials: Critiques and innovations, 713
Cataloguing Wagner, *676*
The Cecil Sharp Library: The story of the library, its contents, services, and classification scheme, 174

Title Index

A census every month (*Schwann catalog*), *156*
Ceskoslvensko, *380*
Chamber music classification scheme: Modification of Altmann's Kammermusik Katalog (1931), *877*
Checklist for cataloguing music manuscripts and prints, *457*
Choice of main entry for sound recordings, *550*
Chorlist: Computerized index to choral octavo scores, *564*
Class M, music and books on music (combined schedule through 1991): Library of Congress classification schedules combined with additions and changes through 1991, *802*
Class M, music and books on music (cumulation through 1992): Library of Congress classification schedules: a cumulation of additions and changes through 1992, *812*
Class M: music and books on music. SuperLCCS: Gale's Library of Congress classification schedules combined with additions and changes through 1993, *822*
Class M—Music; Class ML—Literature of music; Class MT—Music instruction, *6*
Class numbers for records, *443*
Classement d'une bibliothéque musicale par F.-J. Fétis, *221*
Le classement par incipit musicaux, *190*
Classification and cataloging, *336*
Classification and cataloging of music scores in libraries, *92*
Classification and cataloging of spoken records in academic libraries, *355*
Classification and cataloguing of music in public libraries, *32*
The classification and cataloguing of sound recordings: An annotated bibliography, *534*
Classification, cataloging, indexing, *160*
Classification chaos, *288*
Classification Class M: Music and books on music, *554*
Classification. Class M, Music; Class ML, Literature of music; Class MT, Musical instruction, *13, 14*
Classification de las obras de musica, *871*
A classification for Baroque music, *407*
Classification for music scores on historical principles, *281*
Classification for music scores used in the Chicago Public Library, *872*
Classification in American music libraries, *93*
Classification of folk music and dance (with relevant subjects) prepared for the Cecil Sharp Library, *88*
Classification of four track tapes, *249*

Classification of literature: Classification of music, 875
Classification of music, *113*
Classification of music: Analyzing and classifying music for hospital repertoire and general rules for using it, *130*
The classification of music and literature on music, *382*
Classification of musical compositions: A decimal-symbol system, 36
The classification of nonbook materials in academic libraries: A commentary and bibliography, 448
Classification problems in bibliographies of literature about music, *73*
Classification research: Proceedings of the Second International Study Conference, 317
Classification scheme: Long playing records, 158
Classification schemes for scores: Analysis of structural levels, *814*
Classificazione e musica. DDC-proposed revision of 780, music, *691*
A classified catalogue of musical scores: Some problems, *111*
Classifying phonograph records using the Dewey decimal classifications: A section of the Edmonton Public Library cataloguing manual, 358
The co-operative "Muziek catalogus Nederland", *707*
Code for cataloging music and phonorecordings, 183
Code for cataloging music: preliminary version issued by chapters, 56
Code for cataloguing music, *47*
Code for classifiers, 133
Code international de catalogage, *171*
Code international de catalogage de la musique, 173
Code restreint, 233
Collecting gramophone records, 246
Collectors, catalogs and libraries, *503*
Coloured cards for music in the Bodleian, *303*
Command performances: phonorecords related to books and classified, 172
Comment: Miles, R. Cataloging and classification of music on phonorecords: Some considerations, *496*
Comment nous utilisons l'electro-mécanographie, *167*
Commission de travail, *444*
A comparison of PRECIS and Library of Congress subject headings for the retrieval of printed music, 717
Computer aids in music libraries and archives, *571*
Computer cataloguing and the broadcasting library, *538*
Computer-generated cataloging projects in the International Piano Archives at Maryland, *685*

Computereinsatz in der Musikkatalogisierung im Deutschen Rundfunkarchiv, *603*
Computerized cataloging project for archival sound recordings, *474*
Computers, cataloguing, and co-operation, *395*
Condensation of the Library of Congress classification schedule, *287*
Conrad's record index, *98*, *144*
Contemporary music at Trinity and All Saints College, *622*
The core bibliographic record for music and sound recordings—working group report from the 1997 IAML Conference, *846*
Critical essays on Nippon decimal classification, proposed 9th edition "arts class," *810*
Critiques: A cataloging technique and a computer aided system for retrieving information about brass music, *439*
Current resources for the bibliographic control of sound recordings, *456*
Czech music libraries, *627*

Da capo, *238*
Dating engraved music: The present state of the art, *437*
Datorbaserad Katalogisering av Grammofonskivor, *438*
DDC, Dewey decimal classification proposed revision of 780 music: Based on Dewey decimal classification and relative index, *584*
De tryckta katalogkorten i teori och praktik, *344*
Debat: g-Seddelfortegnelsen, *391*
Denmark, *388*
Describing jazz, blues, and popular 78 RPM sound recordings: Suggestions and guidelines at Indiana University, Bloomington, *868*
Describing music materials: A manual for descriptive cataloging of printed and recorded music, music videos, and archival music collections, for use with AACR2 and APPM, *844*
La description des archives de musique: Un exemple Canadien—Music Division of the National Library of Canada, *830*
The descriptive cataloguing of music in Japan, *737*
Descrizione della musica a stampa fra ISBD (PM), AACR2 e AACR2 R, *775*
Designing an expert system to assign Dewey classification numbers to scores, *751*
Deutsche Demokratische Republik, *384*
Die deutsche Musik-Phonothek Phonoprisma, *366*
Deutschland: Bundesrepublik Deutschland, *385*
Developing and selecting cataloging systems for private collections, *836*

96 Title Index

The development of a classification for non-Western music: A modification of Library of Congress class M, *716*
Development of library collections of sound recordings, *572*
Developments in the organisation of non-book materials, *532*
The Dickinson classification: A cataloging and classification manual for music: Including a reprint of the George Sherman Dickinson classification of musical compositions, *371*
The Dickinson classification for music: An introduction, *446*
Direct and digital sound recordings: Basics for librarians, *681*
Discography: Its prospects and problems, *570*
A discotopology primer, *620*
Discussion on classification of music by members of the Massachusetts Library Club, *2*
Discussion on the catalogue of the Boston Library, *3*
Disk on the desk, *668*
Documentation sonore et la phonothèque du Musée de la Parole de l'Université de Paris, *30*
Documents musicaux, *809*
Don't knock it 'til you try it—OCLC recently released two CD-ROM music databases: The Music library and the Music cataloging collection, *771*

E dopo Sartori? Considerazioni sulla catalogazione dei libretti, *837*
EDB-Registrering af Grammofonplader, *402*
The effectiveness of keyword searching in the retrieval of musical works on sound recordings, OPAC retrieval techniques, *800*
Efforts in West German Radio to harmonize cataloguing instructions, *455*
Einige Bemerkungen zum EDV-Project bibliographienherstellung der Deutschen Bücherei, *656*
Einordnung im Autorenkatalog der Musikdrücke, *106*
Empfehlungen für eine zeitgemässe Katalogisierung von Musikhandschriften, *274*
En tematisk katalog med numericode-ett projekt vid SMA, *379*
Encore to the *Lexicographer's dilemma*, or de Lalande et du bon sens, *634*
Enhancing nonbook cataloging for online catalogs, use of contents notes for music cataloging, *729*
Enkele kanttekeningen bij de beschrijvings regels voor gedruke muziek, *645*
Entre silence et cacophonie: Le catalogage informatisé des phonogrammes, *821*

Title Index

España, *377*
Establishing an index of musical instruments and musical subjects in works of Western art: Some personal suggestions, *484, 485*
An examination of the music headings in the Library of Congress subject headings, *819*
An expandable classification scheme for phonorecord libraries, *400*

Films and sound records, *152*
Finns det utrymme for specialservice? Problemet idealitet contra lonsamhet diskuteras med exempel fran produktionen av katalogkort till grammofonskivor, *360*
Flexibilis zenei osztalyozasi rendszer: Keigeszitesi javaslatok az apparatus jelzetelesehez, *733*
A flexible classification system of music and literature on music, 383
Foreign-language musical uniform titles required by AACR2, *671*
Form- und Gattungsnamen im Sachkatalog der musica practica: Zum Entwarf eines thesaurus, *619*
Four hundred arts and types of art: A classified list, *168*
Fragen der statistischen Erfassung von Musikalien, *632*
France, *387*
The frequency of personal name headings in the Indiana University Music Library card catalogs, *699*
From Schmidt-Phiseldeck to Zanetti: Establishing an international cataloguing code for music, *356*

Ge oss regler für notkatalogisering (letter), *559*
Good enough for jazz; or, Successful music cataloging for non-musicians, *860*
Gramophone record catalogues, *86*
Gramophone record catalogues based on EDP routines: A short survey, *482*
Gramophone record libraries: Their organization and practice, 273, 414
Graphemic, morphological, syntactical, lexical and context analysis of the Library of Congress music subject headings and their relationship to the Library of Congress classification schedule, class M, as determined by a comparative sampling of their two vocabularies, *440*
Great Britain, *372*
Grund laggande katalogregler for svenska diskotek, 256
Grundzüge einen analytischen Systems der Sachkatalogisierung der "Musica Practica," *166*

Guide for dating early published music: A manual of bibliographical practices, 481

Haandbog i musikbiblioteksarbejde, *566*
A half-million records (BBC Gramophone Library of Commercial Records), *150*
Hankalat musiikkinimet: Ohjeluettelo musikin luetteloinnissa ja tiedonhaussa käytettävistä nimimuodoista, *827*
Have you a catalogue of your music library?, *100*
Heart of the music library, *120*
Heartaches by the number: Cataloging country music at the Country Music Foundation library, *795*
A history of the Archive of Folk Song at the Library of Congress: The first fifty years, *644*
Hudba jako predmet sdeleni, *461*
Hudebni prameny a jejich zpracovani, *339*
The humanities and the library: Problems in the interpretation, evaluation and use of library materials, 155

IJS jazz register and indexes: A COM catalog of the recorded sound collection of the Rutgers Institute of Jazz Studies, *596*
The IJS jazz register and indexes: Jazz discography in the computer era, *647*
The impact of non-book materials—with particular reference to music libraries, *555*
Improving access to music: A report of the MLA Music Thesaurus Project Working Group, *742*
In celebration of Revised 780: Music in the Dewey decimal classification ed. 20, 773
An index of folksongs contained in theses and dissertations in the Library of Congress, Washington, D.C., *613*
Indexing gramophone records, *228*
Indexing rap music literature: An experiment into the creation of a rap music database using *The source: The magazine of hip-hop music, culture, and politics, 859*
Indexing system can catalogue 10,000 records, *431*
Indian music: Expasion [sic] therefore of D. C. schedules, *177*
"Indicators", *420*
The information community: An alliance for progress, 615
An information retrieval system for sound recordings, 299
Information zur Systematik für Musikschallplatten, *502*

Title Index

Inside LC's Music Section, *373*
International Association of Music Libraries, troisième congrès international des bibliothéques musicales Paris, *122*
International code for cataloging music, *229*
Internationale Kommission für Katalogisierung von Musikalien, *184*
ISBD for sound recordings in Poland: Paper given at IAML Congress in Stockholm, August 1986, *720*
ISBD (Music): First meeting of the IFLA/IAML Working Group in Mainz, 29-21 September 1977, *553*
ISBD (Music) progress reported, *545*
The ISBD (NBM) revision: An historical review, especially as it describes sound recordings; presented at the 1988 IAML conference, *748*
ISBD (NBM)—Sound recording: Amendments and additions, *605*
Issues in retrospective conversion for a small special collection: A case study, Moravian Music Foundation, *841*
Italia, *375*

"Jam tomorrow": The present and future state of the British Library's automated music catalogues part 1, *769*
"Jam tomorrow": The present and future state of the British Library's automated music catalogues part 2, *761*
Jazz and reggae at Trinity and All Saints College, *621*
Jazz record collecting—A hot romance, *549*
Joy of cataloging, *614*

K nekterym otazkam soupisu a popisu starych notovanych kniznichy pamatek, *575*
Kak opisyvat' noty i zvukozapisi, *471*
Kall-och litteraturforteckning i musikvetenskapliga arbeten, *306*
Katalogisering af musikalier og grammofonplader: Tillaef til katalogiseringsregler, *313*
Katalogisering av grammofonskivor, *134*
Katalogisering av musikalier, *40*
Katalogisering av musikalier. En orientering, *91*
Katalogisering av musikalier i folkbiblioteken, *146*
Katalogisieren von Musikalien an den öffentlichen MusikBüchereien, *351*
Katalogisierung von Musik-Tonträgern in einer Rundfunkanstalt, *629*
Katalogl fonoteki konsul'tatsiia, *486*
Katalogowanie plyt, *260*
Keeping track, *425*
Klasifikacia hudby, *314*

Klassifikation av grammofon—Och band-upptagninger: Reviderad och detaljerad uppstallning av klassifikationssystemets avdelning, 257
Klassifikation der Musik von Boetius bis Ugolino von Orvieto, 22
Klassifikation Tonträger/Musik—auch für Kinderbibliotheken, 582
Klassifikationsprobleme bei Musikalien Sachstandsbericht, 594
Klassifikatorische Inhaltserschliessung im Fachgebiet Musik, 801
Klassifikatsiia notnoi literatury po tselevomu nazanacheniiu, 26
Kostnader for katalogisering av grammofonskivor, 408

La Roche College classification system for phonorecords, 321
LC music headings [letter], 447
LCSH and PRECIS in music: A comparison, 697
LCSH for music: Historical and empirical perspectives, 866
Let there be music (but not too soon), 614
Lexicographer's dilemma: (Names with prefixes), 157
Library classification of music: Description and critique of selected systems, 222
Library for organists, 162
The Library of Congress classed catalog for music, 297
Library of Congress subject headings for recordings of Western nonclassical music, 679
Librettos, 29
List of uniform titles for liturgical works of the Latin rites of the Catholic Church, 497, 623

Making of a code: The issues underlying AACR 2, 598
Manual de classificação e catalogação de discos musicais, 78
Manual for the cataloging of recordings in public libraries, 307
Manual for the classification and cataloging of music scores, 136
Manual for the classification and cataloging of music scores: The Vassar-Columbia classification scheme integrated with the cataloging procedure manual of the Columbia University Music Library, 137
Manual for the descriptive cataloging of music in the Denver Public Library, 97
Manual of examples of music cataloging, 548
Manual of music librarianship, 336, 335
The MARC format: From inception to publication, 664
MARC tagging workbook: Scores, 601
MARC tagging workbook: Sound recordings, 602
Maschinelle Erfassung und Erschliessung von Musikdaten, 651
The media index: Computer-based access to nonprint materials, 628

Title Index 101

Messkataloge im Dienste der musikalischen Geschichtsforschung: Eine Anregung zur zeitgenossischen Bücherbeschreibung, 319
Metadata for music: Issues and directions, *862*
A methodology for the description and classification of Anglo-American traditional tunes, *359*
Methodology of music theory: a typology of the methods of investigation, classification, and arrangement of musical materials, *123*
More news from OCLC, *746*
Musaurus: A music thesaurus, 782
MUSCAT: A music cataloging inquiry system from California, paper presented at SCIL '88, *734*
Music, *7, 467, 468*
Music: A MARC format, 522
Music and phonorecord code criticized, *175*
Music authority files at the Library of Congress, *581*
The music catalog as a reference tool, *218*
Music cataloging in a public library: Abridged, *58*
Music cataloging in academic libraries and the case for physical decentralization: A survey, *715*
Music cataloging in the Copyright Office, *96*
Music cataloging policy in the General Libraries, 689
Music cataloging problems in a university library: Abridged, *57*
Music cataloging: The bibliographic control of printed and recorded music in libraries, 752
Music cataloging, with an annotated bibliography of useful reference sources, *68*
Music cataloguing and the future, *813*
Music cataloguing at the Toronto Public Library, *64*
The Music Cataloguing Committee at Brussels (IAML), *149*
Music cataloguing: Printed music and sound recordings, paper presented at the annual seminar of the LA Cataloguing and Indexing Group, April 1986, *726*
Music classification, 95, 189, 873
Music classification. Literature of music. Collections of music. Scores of individual composers, 879
Music classification numbers (extract from *Cataloging Service Bulletin 90*), *432*
Music classification used at Toledo, 880
Music code, *55*
Music coding and tagging, 772
Music collection in American libraries: A chronology, 616

Music goes on-line: Retrospective conversion of card catalog records for music scores at Morris Library (SIU-C), *684*
Music in an automated cataloguing system using MARC, *469*
Music in libraries, *8*
Music in medium-sized libraries, *327*
Music in public libraries, *9*, *19*
Music in the catalog department of a small college library, *112*
Music in the Dewey decimal classification, *527*
Music in the library: A comparative analysis of several classification schemes, *597*
Music in the OCLC online union catalog: A review, *637*
Music in the OCLC online union catalog: A review erratum, *638*
Music librarianship, *573*
Music librarianship: A practical guide, *191*, *694*
Music librarianship at the turn of the century: Cataloging, *869*
Music librarianship in the United States, *640*
Music, libraries and instruments: Papers read at the Joint Congress Cambridge, 1959 of the International Association of Music Libraries and the Galpin Society, *227*
Music libraries, *33*, *323*, *558*
Music libraries and a subject heading code, *803*
Music libraries cooperate on retro conversion project, *718*
Music Library Association, *48*
The Music Library Association: The founding generation and its work, *617*
Music literature and scores together, expanded and modified from Dewey, *780 870*
Music OCLC recon: The practical approach, *721*
The Music OCLC Users Group tagging workbook and reference manual, *595*
Music of ethnic and national groups, *606*
Music retrospective conversion at the University of California at Berkeley: Conversion of musical scores through a consortium: Presented at the 1988 ALA Conference, *754*
Music schedules of the decimal classification: A historical and critical study, *169*
Music scores at the University of Montana, *138*
Music scores: Retroconversion or recataloging? at Wichita State University Music Library, *805*
Music: Special characteristics for indexing and cataloguing, *826*

Music subject heading system: The outline of an expansive decimal system for a logical classification of musical literature, 24
Music subject headings, 71, 728, 850
Music subject headings: A comparison, 477
Music subject headings authorized for use in the catalogs of the Music Division, 196, 345
Music subject headings from the machine-readable Library of Congress subject authority file, 732
Music subject headings used on printed catalog cards of the Library of Congress, 110
Music symbols and online catalogs: A survey of vendors and an assessment of retrieval capabilities, 794
The music thesaurus: Functions and foundations, 817
The Music Thesaurus Project at Rutgers University, 824
The music uniform title: Sources for the novice cataloger, AACR2 chapter 25 rules, 739
Musica nelle norme italiane di catalogazione, 690
Musical bumps: Indexing musical terms, 750
Musical functions and bibliographical forms, 520
Musical information services of the British Museum, 165
Musical scores and recordings, 140
MUSICAT: A method of cataloguing music manuscripts by computer, as applied in the Danish RISM Manuscript Project, 525
MUSICAT: A technical description of the Danish Music Cataloguing Project, 536
Musiikiaineiston hakuelementit muotoutuvat, 652
Musik, EDB og gtode programmorer, 526
Musik pa bibliotek: En handbok for det dagliga arbetet, 418
Musikalien im Schlagwortkatalog, 735
Musikalien-Zentralkatalog und Musikalien-Leihverkehr: Planungsgutachten zur Einrichtung eines bundesweiten Leihverkehrs für Musikalien auf der Grundlage eines Musikalien-Zentralkatalogs der Musikbibliotheken der Bundesrepublik Deutschland, 678
Musikalienkatalogisierung; ein Beitrag zur Lösung ihrer Probleme, 20
Musikdebat: Gruppe 78 i DK 5. udgave; nogle kritiske bemaevkninger, 423
Musikkbibliotekarene venter pa ny oversettelse av katalogiseringsreglene, 631
Musikkbiblioteket: Hjelpebok for bibliotekarer, 266
Musikkiiluettelointi harhailee, 537

Musikleben und Musikbibliothek: Beiträge zur musikbibliothekarischen Arbeit der Gegenwart, vorgelegt anlaesslich des 75-jaerigen Bestehens der oeffentlichen Musikbibliothek in Frankfurt am Main, 583
Musiksonderregeln zu den Regeln für die alphabetische Katalogisierung, *650*
Musique à la BCU de Lausanne, *394*
Musique dans SIBIL—Lausanne integrated library system, *811*
Musique imprimée, *820*
Must we have that new look in music subject headings?, *72*

'N praktiese benadering van die katalogisering van plate in 'n onderwyskollegediskoteek, *245*
Naar eenheid in het catalogiseren van muziekwerken, *262*
Nailing Jell-o to a tree: Improving access to 20th-century music, *848*
Name headings with references, *489*
Name pattern of indian musicians and choice of entry element, *539*
National Online Meeting proceedings 1989, New York 9-11 May, *751*
The national plan for retrospective conversion in music, *692*
The nature of music and some implications for the university music library, *511*
Neither book nor manuscript: Some special collections, *406*
Neither fish nor fowl nor good red meat: Using archival descriptive techniques for special format materials—experience of the Center for Popular Music at Middle Tennessee State University, *832*
Nekotorye osobennosti modele bibliograficheskoi zapisi i sistemy kodirovanila notnykh izdanii, *480*
Neues System für Registratur und Archiv, *530*
A new development in printed catalog cards for records, *429*
New numericode thematic catalogue in the library of the Royal Swedish Academy of Music in Stockholm, *551*
Non-musical collections, *176*
Nonprint cataloging for multimedia collections: A guide based on AACR2, *662*
Nonprint materials in the OCLC data base, *515*
Norme di catalogazione della musica a stampa: Una panoramica internazionale, *762*
Not in the B.U.C.: Lost in a binder's collection, *318*
A note on the classification of sixteenth-century music, *109*
Notes for music catalogers: Examples illustrating AACR2 in the online bibliographic record, *816*

Notes of some pioneers: America's first music librarians, *703*
Notes on catalogs and cataloging in some major music libraries of Moscow and Leningrad, *232*
Notes on improvement of the indexing of musical themes, *626*
Notes used on catalog cards, *290*
Notes used on music and phonorecord catalog cards, *252*
Nouveau système de description instrumentale et vocale pour le catalogage des partitions—reprinted from Ecouter-voir, *852*
Now where did I put that Franck Sonata?, *398*
Nuevas normas para la catalogación de los manuscritos musicales: Una propuesta italiana, *712*
The numbers racket, *516*
Nya katalogiseringsmetoder vid Sveriges Radios (SR:s) grammofonarkiv, *465*

O katalogowaniu nagran muzycyncych, *312*
Of music and indexing, *756*
Om klassificering og opstilling af grammofonplader, *403*
On classifying sheet music, *421*
On degressive music bibliography, *867*
On filing records, *397*
On first looking into Dewey decimal classification 20, class 780: A review article, *787*
On LC music headings, *473*
On the future of the Library of Congress classification, *317*
On the occasion of Freddy Larsen's critical remarks on group 78 in DK 5th ed.: Reply, *413*
The online public access catalog and music materials: Issues for system and interface design (ILLINET Online at the University of Illinois at Urbana-Champaign), *804*
Open session on ISBD (NBM), Salzburg 4 July 1979, *592*
Opracowanie rzeczowe zbiorow muzycznych, *324*
Order out of chaos, *195*
Organising music in libraries, *561*
Organizacja i inwentaryzacja zbiorow muzycznych, *235*
Organization of recorded sound, *404*
Organizing jazz records: A listener's viewpoint, *547*
Organizing music in libraries, *346, 347, 600*
Organizing music in libraries vol. 1: Arrangement and classification, *556*
Organizing music in libraries vol. 2: Cataloging, *579*

Organizing the Brevard College Music Library, *492*
Organizing the instrumental music ensemble library with the aid of a machine-assisted system, *653*
Organizing your music library, *463*
Outline of classification for recordings, transcriptions and types, 878
An outline of the disc recordings library of Columbia Broadcasting System, 51

Paraprofessional involvement in music cataloging: a case study in the University Libraries at California State University, Northridge with OCLC member-input copy, *765*
Pass the platters, please, *115*
Patterns of growth in public music libraries, *201*
Pepys ballads, *340*
Perpetual inventory key to efficient record system, *105*
Petty codes and pedagogues, *89*
Philosophy and practice of phonorecord classification at Indiana University, *396*
The philosophy of classification and of classifying, *43*
Phonograph record classification at the United States Air Force Academy Library, *328*
Phonograph record classification schedule, 309
The phonograph record collection. Part 2: Technical notes, *259*
Phonograph record libraries, 415
Phonograph record libraries: Their organisation and practice, 417, 420
Phonograph records in the library, *25, 28*
Phonorecord cataloging: Methods and practices, *182*
Phonorecord classification, *452*
Phonorecords, *119*
Pianoforte music and the decimal classification, *87*
Pictures invade the catalog, *70*
Platebiblioteket i NRK — over 100,000 plater, *639*
Plea for a British union catalogue of old printed music, *61*
Policies of cataloging and classification in self-contained music libraries, *41, 42*
Polish work on the standard bibliographic description for printed music, *666*
Polska, *381*
Populärmusik in der Musikalien-Freihandsystematik—Ein Konzept, *743*
Prefatory note, *14*

PREMARC: Retrospective conversion at the Library of Congress, paper given at the IAML Congress in Stockholm, August 1986, *722*
A primer of non-book materials in libraries, 181
Printed cards for phonograph records, *49*
Printed cards for phonorecords, *124*
Printed cards for phonorecords: Subject headings, *116*
Printed music and the MARC format, *517*
Printed music in the British Museum: An account of the collections, the catalogues, and their formation up to 1920, 574
Probleme bei der Katalogisierung alter Musikdrücke im Lichte der Formate RISM und US-MARC, *856*
Probleme der musikbibliographischen Terminologie, *178*
Problems in applying AACR2 to music materials, *660*
Problems of an international gramophone record catalogue, *145*
Problems of record cataloguing, *240*
Problemy katalogowania alfabetycznego drukow muzycznych, *364*
Proceedings: International Computer Music Conference, Montreal, 1991, 781
Proceedings of the Institute on Library of Congress Music Cataloging Policies and Procedures, 490
Proeve tot het opstellen van een titelbeschrijving voor oude muziekhandschriften, *129*
Prologomena do klasyfikacji ethnomuzykologicznych, *348*
Proposals towards the cataloguing of gramophone records in a library of national scope, *102*
Proposed alternate scheme for Dewey M780, *94*
A proposed information retrieval system for sound recordings, *320*
The proposed revision of 780 music: A reply, *665*
The proposed revision of 780 music and problems on the development of faceted classification for music, *655*
A proposed standard discographical data sheet, *487, 475*
Proposition de classification décimale pour les besoins des bibliothéques musicales de type multimedia, *730*
Providing access to a collection of recorded music at the University of North Carolina at Chapel Hill's student radio station, WXYC-FM, *823*
Public library phonorecord system, *458*
Punched card gramophone record catalogue at Luton Central Library, *341*

A question of identity, *501*

108 Title Index

Quick reference classification code for non-music records; For music records, 874

Re-cataloging a college score and phonorecords collection, *427*
Reader in music librarianship, 462
Recent changes in computer and electronic music subject headings at the Library of Congress, *781*
Record cataloguing, *163, 153*
Record collections, *214*
Record industry notes, *449*
Record Libraries Commission, *521*
The recorded programmes libraries of the BBC, *251*
Recordings field guide, 658
Recordings in the high school library, *326*
Recordings in the public library, 285
Recordings of non-Western music: Subject and added entry access, 535
Records ain't what they used to be: Record classification, *450*
Records at your fingertips, *108*
Records: How to arrange your collection, *518*
Records to enrich the teaching of languages, *185*
Regeln für die alphabetische Katalogisierung der Musikalien, 254
Regeln zur Katalogisierung in der Deutschen Bücherei eingehenden Musikalien, 186
Regels voor de titelbeschrijving en schema van een systematische Indeeling van muziekwerken, 46
Regler for klassificering og opstilling af grammofonplader, *367*
Regole di catalogazione della musica e dei documenti sonori, *593*
Relationship of the IAML cataloguing code to the newly completed ISBD (PM and NBM) and AACR2: A preliminary study of the need and the feasibility of revising the IAML cataloguing code in the light of these developments, *663*
Répertoire iconographique de l'opera (RICO), *389*
Report—Committee for Cataloging and Filing Phonograph Records, *52*
Report International Conference on Cataloguing Principles, Paris, 9th-18th October 1961, 277
Report of ALA Committee on Catalog Rules: Rules for Cataloging Musical Scores, *15, 17*
Report on National Program Archives, *428*
Research on nonbook materials undertaken by the British Library, *508*

Retrospective conversion of music materials: Report of a meeting sponsored by the Council on Library Resources, July 18-19, 1984, Wayzata, Minnesota, 687
Revising the Dewey music schedules: Tradition vs. innovation, *648*
Revision of DC 780: The Phoenix schedule, *493*
Revision RAK-Musik: Abschlußbericht, *833*
RISM-Handschriftenkatalogisierung und elektronische Datenverarbeitung (EDV), *580*
RISM; Sitzung am 27. August 1967 in Salzburg, *378*
Rules for a dictionary catalog, 7
Rules for cataloging music manuscripts, *499*
Rules for cataloging of musical scores, *16*
Rules for descriptive cataloging in the Library of Congress: Phonorecords, *301*
Rules for full cataloging, *435*
Rules for the brief cataloging of music in the Library of Congress: Exceptions to the Anglo-American cataloging rules, *424*
Running a record library, *322*

Säännöistä yhtenäiseen käytäntöön, *711*
Samarbete efterylses!, *147*
Schlagwortkatalog der musikwissenschaftlichen Literatur auf systematischer Grundlage, *23*
Schweiz, *390*
Scores and recordings, *476*
Scores field guide, *659*
Scores format, *709*
The selection, processing, and storage of non-print materials: A critique of the Anglo-American cataloging rules as they relate to newer media, *357*
The Selmer music library manual, *50*
Serving the school radio station, *65*
Sharing information on archival collections: MARC AMC and beyond in the U.S. experience of the Juilliard School and 12 other institutions, *808*
Sheet music cataloging and processing: A manual, *701*
Sheet music cataloguing system for sound recordings, *675*
Shelf arrangement systems for sound recordings: Survey of American academic music libraries, *780*
Shelf classification of music, *4*, *5*
Shelflisting music, *230*

Shelflisting music: Guidelines for use with Library of Congress classification: M, 636
Simple cataloging of audio-visual materials, *76*
Simplified cataloging: Here's one for the record, *325*
Simplified cataloging of music, *81*
Simplified procedures for recordings, *60*
Simplified rules of cataloging of music, *101*
Simplify record classification, *206*
Sink or swim!, *141*
SLACC: The partial use of the shelf list as a classed catalog, 470
Slavic sacred music: Issues in cataloguing—paper presented at the 1997 MLA conference, *843*
Sodaine and unexpected music in the renaissance, *90*
Some current developments in the bibliographic control of music and the British Library's catalogues, *727*
Some information on the cataloging of phonograph records, *219*
Some problems in the cataloging of musical manuscripts and printed scores, *84*
Some pros and cons regarding an international code for cataloging practical music, *122*
Some remarks on the Library of Congress classification schedule for music, *524*
Sonderkataloge für Musiksammlungen: Aus der Praxis einer öffentlichen Hochschulbibliothek, *500*
Sonderregeln für Musikdrücke und Musiktonträger zu den Regeln für den Schlagwortkatalog (RSWK), *797*
Sound archives indexing (of 78s on file), *611*
The sound archives of the Centre for Nigerian Cultural Studies, *670*
Sound archives: The role of the collector and the library, *604*
Sound librarian—The music cataloging tool for Windows, *831*
Sound recording cataloging: A practical approach: Cataloging compact disc recordings issued previously in LP or cassette format: Experience of Dartmouth College Library, *764*
Sound recording vendor offers MARC cataloging, *673*
Sound recordings format, 710
Sound recordings & N.B.M. rules, *464*
Special cataloguing: With particular reference to music, films, maps, serials, and the multi-media computerised catalogue, *467, 468*
Special materials in the library, 269
Specification for the presentation of bibliographical information in printed music, 434

Specificonostmuzike i njeno u klasifikaciji umetnosti, *460*
The spoken recordings: An innovation, *180*
Staff-liner identification: A technique for the age of microfilm, *361*
Standardization of the bibliographic description of printed music in the USSR, *649*
State of record cataloging, *472*
A statement on archiving, *399*
The story of "Nipper" and "His Master's Voice", *680*
Study into the effects of AACR2 on music MARC catalogues: Preliminary report from the BLCMP Music Group, *565*
A study of music cataloging backlogs: Survey of 357 institutional subscribers to the *Music Cataloging Bulletin*, *818*
Study of the music at the Toronto Public Library, *284*
A study of the problems involved in the classification and arrangement of college record collections, *179*
Stuttgarter akzente, *661*
Subject access to archival fonds: Balancing provenance and pertinence, *834*
Subject access to jazz and popular music materials on Library of Congress catalog records, *700*
Subject and technical specialists' cooperation on a score cataloging project, *131*
Subject commission on cataloguing, *847*
Subject headings for Jewish liturgical sheet music used at Hebrew Union College, *792*
Subject heads: A rebuttal (letter), *479*
A suggested list of thematic catalogues and their recommended abbreviations, *745*
Summary report of activities: IAML Project Group on Classification & Indexing, *766*
Suomi, *376*
Supplement for ISBD enthusiasts, *576*
Survival through coordination: The future development of libraries, *624*
Symposium on music in libraries: Contributed by various libraries in the United States, *10*
Syncopation automation: An online thematic index, *654*
A system of classification for music and related material, *135*
Systematic discography, *478*
Systematik der Musikliteratur und der Musikalien für öffentliche Musikbüchereien, *276*

112 Title Index

Systeme de constitution et d'exploitation données pour l'identification et l'analyse de textes musicaux, *514*

Tableau de classification, *370*
Teatro e musica nel soggettario italiano, *686*
Techniques for handling phonograph records, *142*
Thematic catalogue numbers in music uniform titles: An international comparison, *740*
Theoretical considerations in the bibliographic control of music materials in libraries, *702*
Three research libraries convert music materials, *724*
Tonträger-Systematik Musik für öffentliche Musikbibliotheken, *466*
Toward a definition of sheet music, *858*
Toward the ideal archival catalog, *488*
Towards a national program for the retrospective conversion of music records, presented at the 1985 IAML conference, *705*
Traditions and achievements of music libraries and library science in the Polish People's Republic, *577*
Treat records like books, *224, 225*
Treatment of nonbook materials, *121*
The treatment of special material in libraries, *139*
Trends in archival and reference collections of recorded sound, *459*
Trois sources pour les notices de documents sonores, *815*

U. S. RISM libretto project with guidelines for cataloguing in the MARC format, *708*
Über den Musik-Thesaurus und die inhaltliche Erschließung von Musik, *838*
Uniform titles for liturgical works, *491, 510*
Uniform titles for music: An exercise in collocating works, *753*
Uniform titles for music under AACR2 and its predecessors: The problems and possibilities of developing a user-friendly repertoire, *713*
Union catalogue of old music, *126*
United States Army Military Band Library, *99*
United States of America, *374*
Use of automatic indexing for authority control, *618*
The user and the music library, *657*
Using early American hymnals and tunebooks, *416*

Verbundkatalogisierung für Musikalien?, *723*

Title Index 113

Vers un taxonomie de l'art, *442*
Versuche mit einigen neuen Katalogisierungsgrundsätzen, *143*
Victrola records popular, *39*
The visible index method of cataloging phonorecords, *393*
Vorschlag zur Dokumentation über Musik, *31*

Wagakuni ni okeru shichokaku shiryo soshikika no shiteki kosatsu, *828*
The Washington Library Institute (International code for cataloging music), *231*
Waving or drowning?—The growth of the music catalogues in the British Library, *755*
We shall have music, *54*
Weitere Entwicklung der Arbeit an ISBD (PM), ehemals ISBD (Music), *569*
West Sussex catalogue of recorded sounds, *505*
What ISBD is all about, *523*
Worcester Free Public Library gives discs full treatment, *74*
Workflow considerations in retrospective conversion projects for scores: Case studies from seven academic music libraries; presented at a Music OCLC Users Group meeting, Tucson, Ariz., February 1990, *799*
Working group offers review of ISBD for non-book materials, *590*
Working Group on the Core Bibliographic Record for Music and Sound Recordings—appointed at the 1994 IAML Conference, *829*
Working groups: Core bibliographic record for music and sound recordings—report from the 1996 IAML Conference, *840*
World Congress of Universal Documentation, *30, 31*
Wskazowki opracowania plyr gramofonwych w zaresie nagren niemuzycznych, *264*

Your jazz collection, 422

A zenemuvek cimleirasanak nemzetkozi szabalyzata, *236*
Zum Aufbau des Einheitssachtitels für Musikalien und Tonträger—Am Beispiel des Deutschen Musikarchivs Berlin, *612*
Zur Bibliographie und Katalogisierung der Textbücher, *107*
Zur Dokumentation des Musiklebens der Gegenwart, national und international, *633*
Zur Einführung der Klassification für Tonträger/Musik, *560*
Zur Entstehung der Musikalien-sonderregeln zu RAK, *599*
Zur Katalogisierung der Musica Practica, *82*

Zur Katalogisierung mittelalterlicher und neuerer Handschriften, 274
Zur Problematik der Schallplattenkatalogisierung: Gedanken über ein bibliothekarisches Spezifikum, *220*
Zur Systematik der Musikbibliographien der deutschen Bücherei, *237*

Author Index

Ahmad, Rashiduddin, *392*
Allan, Ann G., *774*
Allen, Daniel, *445*
Allison, A. M., *564*
American Library Association Catalog Code Revision Committee and [British] Library Association, *53*
American Library Association. Committee on Catalog Rules, *16*
Amesbury, Dorothy G., *28*
Anderson, James D., *719*
Anderson, Jean, *79*
Anderson, K. H., *204*
Anderson, Sherman, *188, 316*
Andrew, Janet Ruth, *532*
Andrewes, Richard, *509*
Angell, Richard S., *116, 154, 317*
Anker, Oyvind, *40*
Arntsen, Ella, *266, 293, 334, 433*
Asheim, Lester et al., *155*
Aswegen-Badenhorst, J. G. van, *245*
Atherton, Pauline, ed., *317*
Audsley, J., *296*
Aurelle, Elisabeth, *757*
Austin, Derek, *693*
Avram, H. D., *451*
Ayer, Clarence W., *4*

Baader, Peter, *491*
Baer, Eckehard, *612*
Balliett, Melvin, *50*
Barnes, Christopher, *294, 355*
Barnhart, Linda K., *758, 759, 760, 857, 864*
Barriault, Jeannine, *830*
Bartis, P. T., *644*
Bauer, Gerd, *793*
Bauman, Joanne, *831, 839, 865*
Bean, Charles W., *613*
Bellord, Julia, *510*
Benton, Rita, *205, 511*
Berger, Arthur, *156*
Berkshire Athenaeum, *189*
Berman, Sanford, *614*
Berneking, Carolyn, *182*
Bielska, Krystyna, *720*
Bindman, Fred, *545*
Birmingham Libraries Cooperative Mechanisation Project (BLCMP), *565*
Bishop, William W., *17*
Bixler, Paul Howard, *54*
Bjornum, Ove, *413*
Blacker, George A., *475*
Blom, Eric, *157*
Borduas, Jean R., *206*
Borghi, Renato, *775*
Bowles, Garrett H., *533, 615, 674*
Bradley, Carol June, *335, 336, 371, 446, 462, 616, 617, 703*
Brandt, A., *295*
Bratcher, Perry, *721, 728, 806*
Bridgman, Nanie, *190*
Briggs, Geoffrey Hugh, *207*
British Standards Institution, *434*
Broadhurst, T. S., *208*
Brooklyn Public Library, *158, 870*
Brown, Andrew F. David, *463*
Brown, G. D., *100*
Brown, James Duff, *1*
Bruhns, S. et al., *566*
Brun, Corinne, *852*
Bryant, Eric Thomas, *86, 87, 191, 228, 246, 247, 267, 268, 372, 464, 694*

Bucknum, Mary Russell, *807*
Buenos Aires Biblioteca Nacional, *871*
Bull, Cecil, *138*
Burbank, Richard, *776, 777, 778, 794*
Burbridge, A. E., *296*
Burkett, Jack, *269*
Burnette, Frances, *176*
Bush, Helen E., *71*
Buth, Olga, *476*

California University Library, *270*
Campbell, A. B., *492*
Campbell, Freda, *57, 591*
Canby, Edward Tatnall, *546, 567*
Carey, John T., *393*
Carter, Nancy F., *675, 729*
Cassaro, James P., *813, 847*
Cato, Anders, *840*
Cazeaux, Isabelle, *271, 336*
Chailley, Jacques, *248*
Chailley, Marie-Noëlle, *730*
Chan, T. S., *547*
Chicago Public Library, *872*
Christensen, Inger M., *72*
Cipolla, Wilma Reid, *477*
Claesson, Inge, *465*
Clavel, J. P., *394*
Cleveland Public Library, *873*
Clews, J. P., *493*
Clough, F. F., *145*
Coates, Eric J., *209*
Cobbe, Hugh, *761*
Cody, Jan, *695*
Cohen, Allen, *249*
Colby, Michael D., *704, 779, 848*
Collison, Robert L., *80, 139*
Columbia Broadcasting System, *51*
Coopersmith, Jacob Maurice, *119*
Coover, James B., *192, 395*
Coral, Lenore, *568, 592, 748*

Cosme, Luiz, *78*
Cox, C. T., *210, 211*
Critchley, W. E. G., *272*
Crow, Linda, *780*
Culshaw, J., *512*
Cuming, Geoffrey, *145, 240*
Cundiff, Morgan, *685*
Cunningham, Virginia A., *81, 101, 120, 193, 212, 229, 230, 297, 337, 356, 373, 374, 435*
Cunnion, Theodore, *213*
Currall, Henry F. J., *273, 414, 415, 417, 420*
Currier, Thomas Franklin, *29*
Cutter, Charles Ami, *5, 7*

Daily, Jay E., *357, 494, 495, 496*
Damiani, Maria Raffaella, *762*
Daub, Peggy Ellen, *749*
Davidson, Mary Wallace, *705, 731, 763*
Davies, J. H., *159*
Davis, D. K., *214*
Davis, Deta S., *781*
De Lerma, Dominique-René, *396*
Dean-Smith, Margaret, *88, 102, 103*
Deathridge, J., *676*
Dehennin, W., *129*
Derbyshire, Joseph J., *447*
Deutsch, Otto Erich, *61*
Deutscher Bibliotheksverband. Arbeitskreis öffentliche Musikbibliotheken. Kommission für Tonträger-Systematik, *466*
Devigne, Roger, *30*
Dewey, Harry, *175*
Dickinson, George Sherman, *36*
Dijk, W., *645*
Dillon, Martin et al., *618*
Dona, Mariangela, *375, 593*
Dorfmüller, Kurt, *594, 619, 683*
Dougherty, K., *215*
Dowell, Arlene Taylor, *513, 646, 696*
Drake, Helen, *298*
Drone, Jeanette, *732*

Droste, Kathleen, *802, 812, 822*
Ducasse Henri, *514*
Duck, L. W., *216, 217, 250*
Duckles, Vincent, *140, 231*
Duncan, Barbara, *104*
Dunkin, Paul S., *89*

Eckersley, T., *251*
Edmonton Public Library, *358*
Eick, B., *620*
Elfers, J., *548*
Elliker, Calvin, *814, 858*
Ellison, M., *338*
Ellsworth, Ralph E., *25*
Elmer, Minnie, *58, 68, 160, 218, 232*
Enkstrom, Ann, *515*
Erdelyi, Frigyesne, *733*
Ericksen, Dawn A., *803*
Eskew, Harry, *416*
Eustis, Edwina, *130*
Ezquerro Esteban, Antonio, *849*

Famera, Karen M., *706*
Ferand, E. T., *90*
Finney, T. M., *318*
Flint, J. M., *436*
Foreman, Lewis, *478*
Forslin, A., *376*
Foss, G., *359*
Foster, Donald L., *252, 448*
Free Library of Philadelphia Music Department, *877*
Frisoli, Patrizia, *686*
Frost, Carolyn O., *677*
Fulton, Gloria, *734*
Funabiki, Ruth P., *595*
Fédoroff, Yvette, *233*

Gabbard, Paula Beversdorf, *697*
Gaeddert, B., *534*
Garland, Catherine, *722*
Garrison, Ellen, *832*

Gaschignard, Jean-Paul, *815*
Gavalda, M. Q., *377*
Gee, Mable W., *141*
Geering, M., *569*
Geist, B., *339*
Gemert, Joost van, *707*
Gié, Hélene, *852*
Gnarro, B., *105*
Godfrey, Marlene, *621*
Gohler, Albert, *319*
Goldstein, Leba M., *340*
Goldthwaite, Scott, *73*
Goodfriend, J., *397*
Gorman, Hester, *622*
Gottlieb, Jane, *808*
Gottwald, C., *274*
Grafton, Derek, *417*
Grasberger, Franz, *106*, *107*, *161*, *253*
Gray, Michael, *570*
Graydon, Alec, *516*
Green, Laura Gayle, *799*
Greener, B. R., *374*
Greensboro, N.C. Public Schools, *874*
Gregor, Dorothy, *687*
Griffin, Marie, *596*, *647*
Gross, Linda, *795*
Guerrini, Mauro, *775*

Hagen, Carlos B., *299*, *320*
Halberg, Per, *418*
Hall, D., *449*
Hallgren, Sante, *360*
Hallowell, Jared R., *219*
Hamilton, D., *398*
Hammond, H., *341*
Hammond, Merrill M., *549*
Hanauer, Julius, *31*
Hardeck, Erwin, *678*, *723*, *833*
Harperink, Bernadette, *796*
Harris, K. G. E., *275*
Harrold, Ann, *782*, *793*

Hart, Richard, *176*
Hartman, E. R., *342*
Hartsock, Ralph, *816*
Harvard Musical Association Library, *875*
Haskell, Inez, *62*
Hassell, Robert Hanks, *597, 648*
Hawthorne, Mrs. G. S., *162*
Haykin, David Judson, *71*
Heckmann, Harald, *378, 571*
Held, Naomi Edwards, *688*
Hell, Helmut, *735, 797*
Helmick, C., *163*
Hemmasi, Harriette, *798, 817, 824, 850, 866*
Henderson, Ruth, *479*
Henigman, Barbara D., *794*
Hensel, Evelyn M., *121*
Herrick, M. D., *131*
Herrold, Charles M., *713, 783*
Hess, Albert G., *132*
Heyer, Anna Harriet, *41, 42*
Hieb, Fern, *841*
High, Walter M., *736*
Hill, Richard S., *122*
Hilton, Ruth, *419*
Hingorani, Rattan P., *177*
Hinton, Frances, *598*
Hirao, Kozo, *737*
Hitchon, Jean C., *420*
Hoban, Michi S., *764*
Hoboken, A. van, *178*
Hoek, D. J., *868*
Hoffmann, Frank W., *572*
Hoffmann, H. K., *550*
Holzberlein, Deanne, *738*
Hopkins, J. A., *8*
Horner, John Leonard, *467, 468*
Howard, G., *242*
Howe, J., *108*
Hubbard, Lee, *450*
Humman, Frances, *164*

Inman, Ruth A., *825*
International Association of Music Libraries, *173*
International Association of Music Libraries. Deutsche Gruppe, *276*
International Association of Music Libraries. Landesgruppe Deutsche Demokratische Republik, *254*
International Conference on Cataloguing Principles (1961: Paris, France), *277*
International Federation of Library Associations. Working Group on Uniform Headings for Liturgical Works, *497*, *623*

Jacobson, G. H., *123*
Jander, O., *361*
Jean, Stéphane, *830*
Johansson, Corry, *551*, *876*
Johnson, B. Lamar, *59*
Jones, A., *624*
Jones, Dolly, *738*
Jones, Malcolm, *517*, *573*
Jones, Peter Ward, *552*

Kan, I., *625*
Kaufman, Judith, *535*, *679*
Kemp, M. L., *74*
Kenton, Egon F., *109*
Keyser, P., *518*
Khasanova, N., *486*
King, Alexander Hyatt, *165*, *574*
Kingsbury, Raphaella, *179*
Kinkeldey, Otto, *11*
Kirchberg, Klaus, *519*
Kirstein, Finn, *536*
Kjellberg, E., *379*
Klein, Arthur Luce, *180*
Kleteckova, Marie, *575*
Kobayashi, Mari, *626*
Kohler, K. H., *166*, *220*
Kokkonen, Oili, *537*
Koltypina, Galina B., *480*, *649*
Koonce, Taneya Yvette, *859*
Kossman, F. K. H., *278*

Koth, Michelle, *799*
Kotherova, E., *627*
Kottelwesch, C., *274*
Kranz, Jack, *739, 765*
Krohn, Ernst C., *421*
Krohn, I. K., *380*
Krummel, Donald W., *481, 520, 867*
Kuyper-Rushing, Lois, *851*

Langridge, Derek Wilton, *422*
Lanzke, Heinz, *553, 599, 650*
Lapique Becali, Zoila, *279*
La Roche College Music Department, *321*
Larrabee, B. B., *300*
Larsen, Freddy, *423*
Lawrence, J. E., *564*
Lea, Graham, *782, 793*
Leavitt, D. L., *280*
Leazer, Gregory H., *800*
Lebeau, E., *234*
Lecompte, Yves, *167*
Lellky, Ake, *91*
Lenneberg, Hans, *437*
Lerch, Dieter, *651*
Lewis, D., *521*
Library of Congress, *6, 13, 14, 424, 489, 554*
Library of Congress. Descriptive Cataloging Division, *301*
Library of Congress. MARC Development Office, *522*
Library of Congress. Subject Cataloging Division, *110*
Liebman, Roy, *628*
Limbacher, J. L., *498*
Lincoln, Sister Mary Edmund, *142*
Lindberg, F., *438, 482*
Linden, Albert, van der, *221*
Lindner, Richard John, *439*
Line, Maurice B., *111, 281*
List, George Harold, *399*
Lloyd, Kim, *818*
Lönn, Anders, *740*
Look, Wallace C., *92*
Luke, Karl, *629*

Lundevall, A., *146*
Lunin, Lois F. et al., *615*
Luttman, Stephen F., *860*

MacLeod, Judy, *818*
MacNeil, Heather, *834*
Makela, Kyosti, *652*
Mantz, Stephen Lee, *819*
March, Ivan, *302*, *322*
Martinez-Göllner, Marie Louise, *499*
Maruyama, L. S., *451*
Mason, Donald, *181*
Mason, Eric, *425*
Massil, S. W., *469*
Massip, Catherine, *809*, *820*
Mayson, William Augustus, *653*
Maywhort, Mrs. H. W., *69*
McCleskey, Sarah E., *842*
McClymonds, Marita P., *708*
McColvin, Lionel R., *19*, *32*, *33*, *194*, *323*
McFarland, Roger B., *401*, *452*
McGaw, Howard F., *343*
McKee, Elwood A., *835*, *836*
McKnight, Mark, *741*, *742*
McMullen, H. T., *195*
McPherson, Beryl, *182*
McPherson, Harriet D., *43*
Meikleham, M. H. C., *63*
Merlingen, W., *143*
Merrill, William S., *133*
Meyer-Baer, Kathi, *93*
Meyers, J. A., *826*
Miles, Robert, *483*
Milhous, Virginia Alice, *112*
Millen, Irene, *201*, *362*
Miller, A. Patricia, *654*
Miller, Catharine K., *70*
Miller, Karen, *654*
Miller, Miriam, *426*, *538*
Miller, Philip L., *34*, *255*, *282*, *453*, *454*

Mills, Julia Louise, *54*
Mills, P., *576*
Mills, Patrick, *523*
Minarek, Erwin, *698*
Miura, H., *810*
Moon, Meredith M., *303*
Moor, E. L., *304*
Morgan, T. S., *269*
Moritz, R. G., *75*
Morner, Carl Gabriel Stellen, *134, 256, 257, 258, 283, 344, 363*
Morsch, Lucille M., *124*
Mrygon, Adam, *364*
Mudge, Suzanne, *868*
Mullally, George P., *524*
Müller-Benedict, Markus, *743, 801*
Munro, Thomas, *168*
Music Library Association, *52*
Music Library Association and the American Library Association, Division of Cataloging and Classification, *183*
Music Library Association. Cataloging and Classification Committee, *470*
Music Library Association. Cataloging Committee, *56*
Music Library Association. Committee on Classification, *94, 95*
Musiol, Karol, *235, 324, 381, 500*

Nettl, Bruno, *222*
Neumann, Klaus L., *455*
Nevraev, V. IU., *480*
New York Public Library. Reference Department, *196, 345*
Newbould, Brian, *501*
Nixon, C., *751*
Nolan, John L., *241*
Novikova, Elena Andreevna, *471*

O'Meara, Eva Judd, *44, 55*
Ohm, B., *325*
Ohman, Hazel Eleanor, *24*
Olding, R. K., *135*
Oldman, C. B., *305*
Olsen, Vivian, *724*
Olson, Nancy B., *630*

Olsson, K., *147*
Online Computer Library Center, Inc., *709*, *710*
Opsal, Tua Standahl, *631*

Padgett, L., *751*
Page, A., *64*
Pages, Denys, *514*
Palmer, William W., *284*
Papakhian, Arsen Ralph, *637*, *638*, *699*, *869*
Park, Amey L., *774*
Parmentier, Martine, *821*
Patterson, Charles Darold, *440*
Pavlovsky, Taras, *843*
Pearson, Mary D., *285*
Peck, John G., *169*
Pedley, Mrs. K. G., *65*
Perret, L. D., *394*
Perry, Helga, *750*
Pethes, Ivan, *236*, *382*, *383*
Petts, Leonard, *680*
Pfeiffer, G., *502*
Phillips, Don, *400*
Philp, Geraint J., *655*
Pietro, Sister M., *326*
Pietzsch, Gerhard W., *22*
Pilton, J. W., *259*
Pinion, Catherine F., *555*
Pittsburgh Public Schools, *878*
Plesske, Hans-Martin, *237*, *384*, *656*
Plumb, P., *242*, *286*
Poroila, Heikki, *711*, *827*
Pratt, George, *657*
Price, Harry Howe, *700*, *784*, *785*, *786*
Prokopowicz, Maria, *260*, *577*

Quinly, William, J., *151*

Raccah, Philippe, *821*
Radcliffe College Library, *879*
Rangra, V. K., *539*

Rasmussen, Mary, *484*, *485*
Ravilious, C. P., *578*
Redfern, Brian L., *346*, *347*, *556*, *561*, *579*, *600*, *787*
Reeves, Harold, *33*, *323*
Reimer, Jürgen, *632*
Reinhold, H., *148*
Research Libraries Group, Inc., *601*, *602*, *658*, *659*
Richmond, S., *660*
Riddle, C., *9*
Riva, Federica, *837*
Rklitskala, A., *486*
Robbins, Donald C., *456*
Robinson, S. A., *170*
Rochester, M., *365*
Rogers, Carolyn, *852*
Rogers, J. V., *662*
Rosa Tola de Schwalb, C., *125*
Rosenberg, Kenyon Charles, *472*, *681*
Rösing, Helmut, *580*
Rösner, Helmut, *385*, *661*
Roth, Christine, *811*
Rovelstad, Betsy, *96*, *287*
Ruden, Jan Olof, *306*
Runchok, Rita, *802*, *812*, *822*
Russell, John F., *37*

Saheb-Ettaba C., *401*
Sarno, Jania, *712*
Sass, Herbert, *633*
Sawkins, Lionel, *634*
Schaal, Richard, *223*
Scharff, Mark, *853*
Schermall, H., *366*
Schiodt, Nanna, *402*, *457*, *525*, *526*, *663*
Schmeider, W., *82*, *261*
Schmidt-Phiseldeck, Kay, *20*, *149*, *171*, *184*
Schnapper, Edith G., *126*
Schneider, C., *23*
Schneider, Klaus, *838*
Scholz, Dell DuBose, *307*
Schonberg, H. C., *150*

Schultz, Lois S., *751*
Schuursma, Ann, *766*
Scilken, Marvin H., *458*
Scott, Edith, *77*
Segura Aguilo, Joan, *788*
Seibert, Donald C., *664*
Seibert, Donald C., Jr., *713*
Shane, M. Lanning, *45*
Shanton, Kristina, *861*
Shaw, Sarah J., *701*
Sherlock, M., *66*
Shiere, Lauralee, *701*
Simons, Fanny, *46*
Skrobela, Katherine C., *473*
Smiraglia, Richard P., *635, 636, 637, 638, 682, 702, 714, 752, 753, 844, 854*
Smith, L., *403*
Smith, Ruth S., *557, 725*
Smith, Sidney Butler, *60*
Smith-Nielsen, Claus, *536*
Smolian, Steve, *238, 429*
Snekkenes, Gudrun, *639*
Somerville, Sheila A., *197*
Sommerfield, David, *789*
Sonneck, Oscar George T., *7, 14*
Spalding, C. Sumner, *198, 581*
Spear, Horace L., *487*
Spear, Jack B., *152*
Spence, T., *488*
Spivacke, Harold, *35, 239*
Stajic, Branka, *199*
Stanfield, Mary E., *113*
Stauffer, Suzanne M., *792*
Stein, Jay W., *172*
Stephens, Norris L., *744, 767*
Steszewski, J., *348*
Steuermann, Clara, *558*
Stevenson, Gordon, *288, 327, 459, 503, 504, 640*
Stevenson, W. B., *289, 349*
Stiles, Helen J., *328*
Stoakley, Roger J., *505*

Stoessel, K., *603*
Stow, Charles Edward, *67*
Strange, A., *308*
Studwell, William E., *803*
Sunder, Mary Jane, *404*
Sundin, Tommy, *559*
Swain, Olive, *290*
Swan, J., *604*
Sweeney, Russell, *527, 665*

Tanabe, Hisayuki, *828*
Tanno, J., *386*
Taylor, R. T., *441*
Thomas, Alan R., *350, 790*
Thomas, David H., *768, 853*
Thompson, Annie F., *715*
Tilin, Marian, *224, 225*
Tischler, Hans, *405*
Toledo Public Library, *880*
Tolstrup, Kamma, *726*
Tomaszewski, W., *666*
Towsend, Stella R., *114*
Tracey, Hugh, *83*
Troutman, Leslie A., *804*
Tschierpe, Rudolph, *200*
Tucker, Ruth W., *754*
Turner, Malcolm, *727, 745, 755, 769*

Unger, I., *560, 582*
United States Air Force Academy, *309*
Usher, Caroline Payson, *770*
Uspenskaa, S. L., *26*

Van Ausdal, Karl, *595*
Van Hees, C. C., *645*
Van Patten, Nathan, *84*
Varga, Ildiko, *667, 668*
Varga, Ovidiu, *460*
Vaughn, Evelyn L., *127*
Vellekoop, G., *262*
Vellucci, Sherry L., *845, 855, 862*

Voedisch, Virginia G., *771*
Volek, Jaroslav, *442, 461*
Volkersz, Evert J., *406*
Vollans, R. F., *310*
Von Oesen, Elaine, *76*

Walcott, Ronald, *669*
Walker, Diane Parr, *708*
Wallace, Ruth, *21*
Wallon, Simone, *387, 683*
Wassner, H., *351*
Wassner, Hermann, *583*
Watanabe, Ruth, *641*
Watkins, T. T., *226*
Wegg, M. F., *97*
Weidow, Judy, *689*
Weiland, Sue, *805*
Weiss-Reyscher, E., *38*
Weitz, Jay, *746, 772*
Welcome, Jennie, *115*
Wennering, H., *540*
Werkhoven, H. B. van, *541*
Whitehead, R., *311*
Whiting, Bernard C., *407*
Wienpahl, Robert W., *427*
Winke, R. Conrad, *863*
Winkel, E., *263, 388*
Witten, Jane Daley, *823*
Woakes, Harriet C., *670, 716*
Wojnowska, Elzbieta, *856*
Wolff, H. C., *389*
Woods, R., *428*
Wursten, Richard Bruce, *684, 773, 791*

Young, James Bradford, *717, 866*
Young, Percy, *756*
Youngblood, J. *506*
Youngholm, Philip, *671*

Zanetti, Emilia, *690*

Zecca Laterza, Agostina, *691*
Zehntner, H., *390*
Zielinska, Bozena, *264*, *312*

Keyword Index

Academic libraries *30, 45, 54, 57, 59, 63, 79, 112, 137, 138, 248, 270, 309, 321, 328, 343, 355, 396, 427, 448, 492, 500, 511, 596, 621, 622, 635, 688, 685, 715, 765, 780, 799, 879*
Automation *386, 379, 395, 402, 438, 474, 526, 525, 529, 514, 536, 538, 541, 551, 564, 571, 580, 603, 615, 618, 626, 654, 656, 685, 727, 734, 761, 769, 794, 804, 811, 813, 831, 865*
Book reviews *44, 85, 103, 104, 117, 159, 154, 187, 194, 192, 193, 198, 199, 203, 204, 205, 207, 208, 212, 215, 216, 217, 223, 226, 234, 239, 243, 244, 247, 250, 253, 255, 258, 261, 263, 265, 267, 268, 271, 272, 275, 278, 280, 282, 283, 286, 289, 291, 292, 293, 294, 295, 296, 300, 302, 304, 305, 308, 310, 311, 315, 329, 330, 331, 332, 333, 334, 337, 338, 342, 349, 350, 353, 354, 362, 363, 365, 368, 369, 409, 410, 411, 412, 419, 433, 436, 453, 454, 498, 504, 506, 509, 519, 531, 544, 542, 543, 552, 563, 568, 585, 586, 587, 588, 589, 607, 608, 609, 610, 695, 696, 704, 719, 731, 736, 744, 749, 757, 758, 759, 760, 763, 767, 776, 777, 778, 779, 783, 784, 785, 786, 789, 790, 791, 793, 851, 853, 857, 861, 863, 864*
Cataloging rules *7, 15, 46, 52, 55, 56, 81, 89, 101, 122, 117, 137, 143, 149, 154, 171, 173, 175, 183, 189, 192, 193, 198, 199, 223, 231, 243, 254, 256, 271, 277, 301, 313, 352, 356, 357, 367, 424, 426, 430, 507, 509, 519, 545, 552, 553, 559, 569, 578, 589, 590, 592, 593, 598, 599, 605, 631, 635, 650, 660, 682, 663, 686, 690, 711, 720, 748, 774, 775, 833*
Classification *2, 3, 4, 5, 6, 8, 9, 13, 14, 19, 22, 24, 26, 32, 33, 36, 41, 42, 43, 44, 51, 73, 78, 80, 87, 88, 92, 93, 94, 95, 103, 109, 111, 113,*

123, 125, 130, 133, 135, 136, 137, 139, 158, 159, 160, 162, 168, 169, 172, 174, 177, 179, 190, 206, 209, 212, 213, 217, 221, 222, 230, 234, 236, 249, 257, 266, 270, 276, 279, 281, 287, 288, 297, 309, 314, 317, 324, 328, 330, 331, 332, 333, 336, 337, 340, 343, 346, 347, 348, 354, 355, 358, 359, 367, 368, 369, 370, 371, 372, 374, 375, 376, 377, 380, 381, 382, 383, 384, 385, 387, 388, 390, 396, 400, 401, 403, 404, 405, 407, 412, 413, 416, 419, 420, 421, 423, 430, 432, 434, 440, 441, 442, 443, 446, 448, 450, 460, 461, 463, 466, 470, 476, 483, 492, 493, 496, 502, 518, 524, 527, 534, 544, 547, 554, 556, 560, 561, 568, 572, 573, 582, 584, 594, 597, 600, 607, 636, 648, 655, 665, 691, 698, 716, 730, 733, 743, 751, 752, 760, 763, 766, 767, 773, 777, 779, 780, 787, 789, 791, 801, 802, 810, 812, 814, 822, 828, 870, 871, 872, 873, 874, 875, 876, 877, 878, 879, 880

Descriptive cataloging   *1, 7, 11, 12, 17, 18, 19, 20, 21, 27, 31, 32, 33, 34, 35, 37, 38, 40, 41, 42, 46, 47, 48, 49, 52, 55, 56, 57, 58, 60, 62, 63, 66, 67, 68, 69, 74, 75, 76, 77, 80, 81, 82, 83, 84, 86, 89, 91, 92, 96, 97, 100, 101, 102, 106, 107, 114, 118, 120, 122, 124, 125, 127, 129, 131, 132, 134, 137, 138, 139, 145, 146, 149, 153, 154, 157, 160, 163, 164, 170, 171, 173, 175, 182, 183, 184, 188, 192, 193, 197, 198, 199, 200, 202, 210, 213, 218, 219, 220, 223, 228, 229, 231, 232, 237, 240, 245, 248, 252, 254, 262, 264, 266, 271, 274, 277, 279, 290, 298, 301, 303, 306, 307, 313, 316, 318, 319, 323, 325, 330, 332, 333, 334, 336, 337, 338, 341, 342, 344, 346, 347, 349, 350, 351, 352, 353, 354, 355, 356, 357, 360, 362, 363, 364, 365, 368, 369, 373, 391, 392, 393, 395, 416, 417, 420, 424, 427, 429, 430, 431, 435, 437, 438, 439, 441, 452, 455, 457, 464, 465, 467, 468, 471, 472, 473, 481, 482, 483, 474, 475, 476, 486, 487, 489, 490, 491, 492, 495, 496, 497, 506, 507, 509, 510, 513, 519, 520, 523, 525, 534, 535, 539, 545, 548, 550, 552, 553, 557, 561, 562, 565, 566, 569, 573, 574, 575, 576, 578, 579, 580, 581, 586, 587, 588, 589, 590, 592, 598, 599, 600, 605, 607, 612, 618, 623, 629, 630, 634, 635, 645, 646, 649, 650, 651, 653, 660, 662, 663, 666, 667, 671, 673, 674, 675, 676, 677, 678, 682, 688, 689, 696, 699, 701, 702, 704, 707, 712, 713, 714, 719, 720, 723, 725, 726, 729, 731, 737, 738, 739, 740, 741, 744, 745, 747, 748, 749, 752, 753, 755, 757, 759, 760, 762, 763, 764, 765, 767, 775, 776, 777, 788, 796, 800, 806, 807, 809, 813, 816, 820, 826, 827, 828, 829, 830, 831, 832, 835, 833, 836, 839, 840, 842, 843, 844, 845, 846, 851, 849, 852, 853, 854, 855, 856, 857, 860, 862, 865, 867, 868, 869*

Descriptive cataloging rules   *16, 53, 161, 186, 187, 233, 244, 247, 253, 255, 258, 261, 263, 278, 499, 652, 683*

Discography   *570, 620, 647*

Keyword Index

Librettos *29, 107, 708, 837*
MARC *386, 451, 469, 517, 522, 565, 595, 596, 601, 602, 637, 638, 658, 659, 664, 673, 684, 708, 709, 710, 732, 746, 771, 772, 777, 778, 783, 786, 790, 808, 856*
Music librarianship *10, 50, 99, 155, 191, 227, 335, 462, 530, 558, 563, 577, 583, 616, 617, 624, 627, 633, 640, 641, 643, 657, 661, 694, 703*
Musicology *90, 306, 361, 405, 575, 604, 626, 644*
National libraries *46, 88, 102, 165, 373, 508, 528, 536, 574, 581, 586, 613, 644*
Nonbook materials *45, 59, 70, 76, 77, 121, 151, 152, 164, 181, 241, 269, 357, 448, 452, 468, 508, 515, 528, 532, 542, 555, 590, 592, 598, 628, 630, 662, 677, 729*
Public libraries *2, 3, 8, 9, 12, 58, 64, 66, 69, 74, 97, 158, 189, 201, 268, 276, 284, 285, 307, 351, 358, 458, 466, 608, 609, 610, 870, 872, 873, 880*
Retrospective conversion *687, 692, 695, 705, 718, 721, 722, 724, 754, 799, 805, 818, 825, 841*
School libraries *65, 326, 582*
Scores *4, 5, 7, 14, 15, 16, 17, 18, 19, 20, 27, 31, 33, 37, 38, 40, 44, 46, 47, 55, 56, 61, 66, 68, 82, 84, 87, 92, 96, 97, 101, 106, 111, 122, 126, 129, 131, 135, 137, 138, 140, 146, 162, 166, 170, 175, 178, 183, 184, 192, 193, 198, 199, 221, 230, 235, 252, 254, 266, 274, 276, 281, 287, 297, 303, 313, 319, 327, 351, 353, 364, 383, 392, 416, 421, 424, 427, 437, 457, 463, 471, 476, 480, 481, 490, 514, 517, 520, 525, 548, 553, 559, 561, 562, 564, 569, 573, 574, 580, 586, 589, 593, 599, 601, 619, 632, 636, 642, 645, 649, 650, 651, 653, 659, 663, 664, 666, 678, 682, 684, 701, 702, 704, 709, 714, 723, 726, 755, 762, 775, 797, 799, 805, 814, 816, 820, 828, 840, 844, 846, 849, 851, 852, 856, 858, 867, 870, 872, 873, 875, 877, 879, 880*
Sound recordings *25, 28, 30, 34, 35, 39, 51, 52, 54, 56, 60, 62, 63, 65, 66, 67, 69, 74, 75, 78, 80, 83, 86, 98, 102, 103, 105, 108, 114, 115, 116, 117, 118, 119, 124, 127, 128, 134, 139, 140, 141, 142, 144, 145, 147, 148, 150, 152, 153, 156, 158, 163, 170, 172, 175, 176, 179, 180, 182, 183, 185, 188, 192, 197, 198, 202, 206, 210, 211, 213, 214, 219, 220, 224, 225, 228, 238, 240, 242, 245, 246, 248, 249, 250, 251, 252, 256, 257, 259, 260, 264, 265, 266, 267, 268, 270, 272, 273, 275, 280, 282, 283, 285, 286, 289, 291, 292, 293, 294, 295, 296, 298, 299, 300, 301, 302, 304, 305, 307, 308, 309, 310, 311, 313, 315, 316, 320, 321, 322, 325, 326, 328, 329, 341, 355, 358, 360, 366, 367, 391, 393, 396, 397, 398, 399, 400, 401, 402, 403, 404, 408, 409, 410, 411, 414, 415, 417,*

418, 419, 420, 422, 425, 427, 428, 429, 431, 433, 436, 438, 443, 445, 449, 450, 453, 454, 455, 456, 458, 459, 464, 465, 466, 471, 472, 474, 475, 476, 478, 482, 483, 486, 487, 488, 498, 490, 494, 495, 496, 502, 503, 504, 505, 507, 512, 518, 521, 531, 533, 534, 535, 538, 540, 543, 546, 547, 549, 550, 557, 561, 567, 570, 572, 573, 591, 593, 596, 602, 603, 604, 605, 611, 620, 621, 622, 629, 636, 639, 647, 652, 658, 663, 664, 667, 668, 669, 670, 673, 674, 675, 679, 680, 681, 682, 702, 710, 714, 720, 725, 726, 736, 738, 741, 748, 764, 768, 774, 780, 797, 800, 807, 815, 816, 821, 823, 828, 835, 836, 839, 840, 844, 846, 851, 865, 868, 876, 878

Special libraries *75, 85, 130, 146, 417, 538, 557, 603, 629, 725, 823*

Subject headings *1, 11, 23, 71, 72, 104, 110, 116, 166, 196, 332, 333, 334, 336, 337, 338, 342, 345, 346, 347, 349, 350, 354, 362, 363, 365, 368, 369, 430, 440, 447, 477, 479, 484, 485, 535, 561, 573, 579, 587, 588, 600, 606, 607, 614, 619, 679, 693, 697, 700, 706, 717, 728, 732, 735, 741, 742, 750, 752, 756, 758, 760, 763, 766, 767, 777, 781, 782, 784, 785, 792, 793, 797, 798, 801, 803, 813, 817, 819, 824, 834, 838, 847, 848, 850, 859, 860, 861, 863, 866, 864*

Journal Index

ALA Bulletin, 15, 17, 16, 39
American Library Annual, 12
American Library Association Cataloging & Classification Yearbook, 41, 55
American Record Guide, 238, 831, 839, 865
Annual Review of Jazz Studies, 647
Archival Issues, 832
Archives and Manuscripts, 591
ARSC Journal, 428, 429, 503, 533, 604, 620, 835, 836
Assistant Librarian, 216, 217, 275
Audio, 546, 567
Audiovisual Librarian, 528, 621, 622
Australian Library Journal, 135, 311, 365, 436

Bibliotek, 526
Bibliotekar', 471, 486, 625
Bibliotekarz, 264
Biblioteksbladet, 134, 146, 147, 258, 344, 360, 363, 408, 465, 559
Bibliotheekgids, 129
Bibliotheeksleven, 278
Bibliothekar, 502, 560, 582
Biblos, 253
Billboard, 105, 611
Bogens Verden, 263, 295, 367, 391, 402, 403, 413, 423, 438
Bok og Bibliotek, 40, 631, 639

Bollettino d'Informazioni (Associazione Italiana Biblioteche), 593, 686, 690, 691, 775
Brio, 291, 303, 368, 426, 469, 493, 509, 523, 563, 565, 576, 578, 587, 624, 655, 657, 665, 674, 745, 787
Brussels Museum of Musical Instruments bulletin, 712
Bücherei und Bild, 351
Bulletin d'Informations de l'Association des Bibliothécaires Français, 190, 370, 815, 820, 821
Bulletin de Documentation Bibliographique, 234
Bulletin des Bibliothèques de France, 809
Bulletin of the Association of British Theological and Philosophical Libraries, 510

Cataloging & Classification Quarterly, 696, 702, 721, 736, 739, 744, 753, 758, 759, 764, 765, 767, 768, 783, 799, 800, 807, 848, 851, 866, 868
Catalogue & Index, 464, 527, 726
Catholic Library World, 142, 326
Clavier, 518
Collection Management, 564
College Music Symposium, 386
College & Research Libraries, 45, 59, 226, 294, 343, 355, 504
Colorado Libraries, 860
Council for Research in Music Education Bulletin, 506
Crescendo International, 516
Cum notis variorum, 688

Dansk Musiktidsskrift, 585
Documentaliste, 852
Drexel Library Quarterly, 342

Edmonton [Canada] Public Library News Notes, 259
Educational Music Magazine, 108
Estudis balearics, 788
Ethomusicology, 330

Fenix, 125

Fontes artis musicae, 145, 148, 149, 167, 171, 178, 184, 200, 237, 248, 271, 372, 374, 375, 376, 377, 378, 380, 381, 382, 384, 385, 387, 388, 389, 390, 444, 446, 451, 455, 457, 482, 511, 521, 524, 525, 536, 538, 541, 551, 553, 555, 571, 577, 580, 592, 603, 605, 612, 619, 634, 649, 650, 656, 663, 666, 668, 672, 700, 705, 707, 720, 722, 730, 737, 740, 748, 755, 761, 766, 769, 777, 797, 801, 808, 811, 813, 829, 830, 834, 840, 843, 846, 847, 849, 855, 861, 862
Forum Musikbibliothek, 594, 599, 629, 632, 633, 642, 651, 661, 698, 723, 735, 743, 833, 838, 856

Hi-fi Music at Home, 128
High Fidelity, 150, 153, 156, 163, 195, 398, 431, 512
Hudebni Rozhledy, 339
Hudebni Veda, 461

Illinois Libraries, 127, 298, 325, 684
Indexer, 228, 308, 750, 756, 826
Information Hotline, 508
Information Technology and Libraries, 654, 675, 794
Institute of Professional Librarians of Ontario Quarterly, 445
Instrumentalist, 369, 441
International Cataloguing, 491, 550, 562, 667, 727
International Classification, 793

Jazz Journal, 409
Journal of Academic Librarianship, 715, 749
Journal of Aesthetics and Art Criticism, 168
Journal of Cataloging & Classification, 75, 77, 81, 89, 131, 138
Journal of Documentation, 61, 88, 102, 103, 126, 159, 165, 305
Journal of Jazz Studies, 488
Journal of Library Automation, 618
Journal of Research in Music Education, 117, 187
Journal of the American Musicological Society, 361
Journal of the Folklore Institute, 359, 399
Journal of the International Folk Music Council, 315
Judaica Librarianship, 792
Junior Libraries, 211, 224

Kirjastolehti, 537, 652, 711
Knihovna Vedeckoteoreticky sbornik, 575
Konyvtari-Figyelo, 733

Librarian & Book World, 86, 87, 194, 197
Library, 1
Library and Information Science, 626
Library Association Record, 9, 37, 111, 204, 268, 289, 296, 350, 529, 790
Library (Bibilographical Society), 340, 520
Library Focus, 716
Library Journal, 3, 4, 5, 10, 11, 18, 25, 28, 29, 34, 54, 60, 67, 69, 70, 72, 74, 115, 175, 176, 180, 182, 185, 202, 206, 210, 214, 215, 225, 255, 282, 288, 327, 447, 473, 479, 498, 673, 681, 718, 719
Library Journal/School Library Journal Previews, 472
Library of Congress Information Bulletin, 119, 432, 443, 545, 590, 596, 692
Library Quarterly, 43, 44, 73, 192, 239, 300, 437, 697
Library Resources & Technical Services, 162, 164, 188, 198, 249, 297, 316, 328, 362, 393, 396, 400, 404, 406, 427, 477, 483, 494, 496, 660, 648, 699, 731, 763, 776, 778, 789, 798, 818, 825
Library Review, 310
Library Science with a Slant to Documentation, 485, 539
Library Software Review, 734
Library Trends, 121, 140, 151, 152, 201, 218, 241, 357, 456, 459, 476
Library World, 203, 267, 286, 341, 349
Libri, 281, 247
Louisiana Library Association Bulletin, 741

Magyar Konyvszemle, 236
Matrix, 410
Melody Maker, 411
Mens en Melodie, 262
Music and Musicians, 425
Music Cataloging Bulletin, 430, 581, 606
Music Educators Journal, 354, 607
Music In Education, 544
Music Journal, 120
Music & Letters, 552
Music News from Prague, 627
MUSIC OCLC Users Group Newsletter, 740
Music Reference Services Quarterly, 803, 806
Music Review, 93, 329
Music Teacher, 588, 589
Music Teacher & Piano Student, 100

Music Therapy, 130
Musica, 519, 610
Musical Opinion and Music Trade Review, 501
Musical Quarterly, 90, 109
Musical Times, 157, 332, 405, 543, 586, 676
Musicana, 99
Musik und Kirche, 608
Musikbibliothek Aktuell, 500
Musikforschung, 223, 609
Musikhandel, 530
Musikrevy, 540
Muzyka, 348, 331, 364

Nachrichten (Vereinigung Schweizerische Bibliothekare), 265, 394, 569
NATS, 333
New Jersey Libraries, 824
New Zealand Libraries, 79, 207
Nordisk Tidskrift for Bok-och Biblioteksvasen, 91
North Carolina Libraries, 114, 492, 795, 841
North Western Newsletter, 208, 250, 302
Notes, 35, 47, 49, 52, 71, 85, 96, 104, 116, 118, 124, 132, 154, 193, 205, 212, 229, 231, 232, 243, 280, 318, 337, 356, 373, 395, 412, 416, 419, 421, 449, 453, 454, 474, 484, 531, 568, 570, 617, 635, 637, 638, 641, 643, 695, 703, 704, 708, 742, 757, 760, 779, 784, 785, 786, 791, 814, 817, 853, 854, 857, 858, 864, 867, 869
Notes: Supplement for Members, 84, 94, 95, 101, 160, 230, 287

OCLC Micro, 771
Ohio Association of School Librarians Bulletin, 515
Ontario Library Review, 63, 64, 66
Open, 645, 796

Pacific BinderyTalk, 27
Pacific Northwest Library Association Quarterly, 57, 58, 62, 338
Pakistan Library Review, 392
Phonographic Bulletin, 669, 670, 685
Phonoprisma, 366
Proceedings of the 36th annual Catholic Library Association Conference, 213
Program, 505, 517
Przeglad Biblioteczny, 235, 260, 312

Public Libraries, 2, 774

Record Collector, 98, 144
Record Research, 475, 487
Recorded Sound, 240, 242, 292, 542, 251
Reference Quarterly, 628
Reol Nordisk Bibliotekstidsskrift, 293, 334
Research Libraries in OCLC, 724
Revue Belge de Musicologie, 221
Revue d'Esthetique, 442
Revue de Musicologie, 353, 514
Rivista Italiana di Musicologia, 837

Scandinavian Public Library Quarterly, 433
School Librarian, 304
School Library Association of California Bulletin, 65
School Musician, 463
Scottish Library Association News, 272
Second Line, 549
Singapore Libraries, 547
Slovenska Hudba, 314
Sonneck Society newsletter, USA, 706
South African Libraries, 245
Sovetskaia Bibliografia, 26
Sovetskoe Bibliotekovedenie, 480
Special Libraries, 48, 320, 558
Stereo Review, 397
Student Librarian, 177
Studia musicologica, 244
Suomen Musiikkikirjastoyhdistyksen julkaisusarja, 827
Svensk tidskrift for musikforskning, 306, 379

Technical Services Quarterly, 754, 780, 805
Technicalities, 729, 863
Tidskrift for Dokumentation, 283
Tokoha Gakuen Tanki Daigaku kiyo, 828
Toshokan kai, 810

Unabashed Librarian, 450, 458, 671

Wen-hua chi-k'an, 32

Wilson Library Bulletin, 76, *141*
Wisconsin Library Bulletin, 8

Zeitschrift für Bibliothekswesen und Bibliographie, *261*
Zeitschrift für Musikwissenschaft, *23*
Zentralblatt für Bibliothekswesen, *82, 106, 107, 143, 166, 220*
Zvuk, *199, 460*

About the Authors

Richard P. Smiraglia, Ph.D., is professor at the Palmer School of Library and Information Science at Long Island University in Brookville, New York. He teaches courses in knowledge organization, broadly defined, and in research methods at the doctoral level. He has been with the Palmer School since 1992; prior to that he was assistant professor at Columbia University's School of Library Service, 1986-1992, and music catalog librarian at the University of Illinois at Urbana-Champaign, 1974-1986. He is the author of many books and monographs in the fields of knowledge organization, cataloging, and bibliography. He was editor of the journal *Library Resources & Technical Services* from 1990 to 1996 and the Music Library Association's "Technical Reports" series from 1988 to 1994. He is currently a member of the editorial board of *Cataloging & Classification Quarterly* and editor of the quarterly journal *Knowledge Organization*.

His 2001 monograph, *The Nature of "A Work": Implications for the Organization of Knowledge* was the first monograph-length treatment of the topic of works and their role in knowledge organization. In 2002 he edited *Works as Entities for Information Retrieval*, in which an international panel of authors focus on domain-specific research about works and the problems inherent in their representation for information storage and retrieval. His most recent journal publications include "Authority Control of Works: Cataloging's Chimera?" (*Cataloging & Classification Quarterly* 38n3/4 (2004): 291-308), "The History of 'The Work' in the Modern Catalog" (*Cataloging & Classification Quarterly* 35n3/4 (2003): 553-67), "Works as Signs, Symbols, and Canons: The Epistemology of the Work" (*Knowledge Organization* 28 (2002): 192-202), and "Further Progress in Theory in Knowledge Organization" (*Canadian Journal of Information and Library Science* 26n2/3 (2002): 30-49).

J. Bradford Young, B.M.A., M.M.A., M.L.S., has been music technical services librarian for the Otto E. Albrecht Music Library at the University of Pennsylvania in Philadelphia since 1986. He studied musicology and music bibliography at McGill University in Montreal and the University of Illinois at Urbana-Champaign. From 1979 to 1986 he was a music catalog librarian at the University of Illinois. He has served as chair of the Bibliographic Control Committee and of the Subcommittee on Subject Access of the Music Library Association, and was chair of the American Library Association's Subject Analysis Committee. He served on the editorial board of *Library Resources and Technical Services* and *Cataloging & Classification Quarterly* and has taught graduate courses in bibliographic control at the University of Illinois and Drexel University. He is the author of "Recent Trends in Access to Music Materials" in *Beyond the Book: Extending MARC for Subject Access* (G. K. Hall, 1990), the introduction to *Music Subject Headings* (Soldier Creek Press, 1997), and with Harriette Hemmasi "LCSH for Music: Historical and Empirical Perspectives" in *The LCSH Century* (Haworth, 2000).

Wake Tech Libraries
9101 Fayetteville Road
Raleigh, North Carolina 27603-5696

WAKE TECHNICAL COMMUNITY COLLEGE
3 3063 00143577 4

WN
DATE DUE

GAYLORD — PRINTED IN U.S.A.

MAY '08